REAL, RAW

YOUR LOVING KINDNESS
IS ALL AROUND US

RIGHTEOUS,
ROYAL, REGAL

YOU ARE MORE THAN ENOUGH

HEART

SCRIBE

VIBES

Micah N. Dillon

Heart Scribe Vibes
by Micah N. Dillon

For more information, please visit
www.sendingandmending.com

To contact Micah and/or inquire about booking and speaking, email
micahmendedheart@gmail.com

QR Codes

At the end of each chapter are QR codes to access Micah's prayers and songs.
Scan the QR codes by either placing your smart phone's camera over the QR code
or downloading a QR code reader app on your phone. You will automatically be
redirected to the web page containing the extra content. For help or questions,
please contact micahmendedheart@gmail.com

Published by The Core Media Group, Inc., P.O. Box 2037,
Indian Trail, NC 28079

Cover Design: Ashlyn Helms & Nadia Guy
Interior Design: Nadia Guy

ISBN: 978-1-950465-46-0

Printed in the United States of America.

TABLE OF CONTENTS

ACKNOWLEDGMENTS

Many people have been involved in this project. Without their contributions, this book would probably not be in your hands—at least not in its current state.

I would like to thank Nadia Guy and Ashlyn Helms for the *Heart Scribe Vibes* cover, interior, album, and gear designs. Throughout this process, I've learned that a vulnerable heart sparks creative art. Your God-gifted ability to take my word pictures and turn them into beautiful visual art has brought so much joy to my heart.

I would also like to thank Kevin Horner, who worked with me late into many nights and adapted to my crazy schedule as a single mom to build this work from the heart to the page with grace. You have been a wonderful and very patient soul, which has been a gift to me. This book would not have been possible without your master word-building skills. Your input, insight, and guidance have elevated all my heart scribing moments along the way into this finished work I hold in my hand today. To say I'm grateful is an understatement.

To Benjy Johnson and Earthtones Recording Studios, thank you for allowing me to put these songs to flight. You have been so kind and encouraging to me along this new adventure called artistry. We have the same birthday and your name is also my former husband's, and for that I knew this was a gift from heaven. This partnership will have eternal impact. It's been a joy working with you.

To The Core Media Group, you are an AMAZING team who God hand-picked for me. This was a match made in heaven, and I am eternally grateful for all the time, energy, and prayers you have given to see this vision to the finish line. Thank you for holding my hand along the way and for being a lifeline through a very unique storyline.

Thank you to my family, church family, friends, and community—you have helped my healing process throughout this journey. Your acts of kindness, prayers, and encouragement have propelled me forward and sustained me through difficult days. And for that, I am eternally grateful.

To my children I dearly love, Stone and Stella, you are my treasures from the Father above. Thank you for your love, your life, and your grace—you've both taught me more about God (and myself) than you may ever know.

To Yahweh, my Creator, the Father of Light, thank You for speaking to and through my heart. Thank You for creating me, knowing me, loving me, and pursuing me. You are the reason I have any words to say at all. You are my Heartbeat, my Treasure Holder, my Ray of Light, and my Lifeline.

All of you are a part of this book, for each of you has been on this journey with me too.

-THANK YOU ♡

PROLOGUE

HEART SCRIBE VIBES

On April 18, 2017, I attended a Bethel Music concert at Rock Church International in Virginia Beach, Virginia, for my best friend's birthday. At the concert, another friend of mine, Joy, found me. She had a message.

"Micah, it's time for you to get out of your head," Joy said. "It's time for you to write."

I don't know about you, but in my life, I've learned to take those "out-of-the-blue messages" seriously. I wasn't about to ignore that word from my good friend. Two days later, I sat down at my sister's piano, and a melody started coming:

For the Joy of the Lord
Renews my strength
The Joy of the Lord,
The Joy of the Lord is my strength

I couldn't believe it. Within minutes, I had the chorus and the beginning of my first song called "The Joy of the Lord." I didn't have the verse yet, but I had the revelation, the resolve of it—and that was miles ahead of anything I'd written to that point.

About a month later, the verse came. I was listening to an episode from Jonathan and Melissa Helser's podcast, "The Presence is Greater than the Pressure." In the podcast, Jonathan talked about how God's presence enables us to overcome pressures that arise in our lives. I don't know how exactly—that's the serendipity of creating art—but the faith in Jonathan's teaching inspired me. I had the verse:

> *I look to You for help*
> *For the pressures of life*
> *Bear down on me*
> *I look to You for help*
> *So let Your presence come*
> *And blow through me*
> *Let Your presence come*
> *'Til I am free*

Something felt so sweet about that song—I'd never experienced anything like it. Something just clicked. I thought ahead to our church's annual anniversary services coming up that June. As the worship leader, I just knew I needed to have this song ready by then. I felt a nudge from Yahweh. A lot happened in those next two months to make this a reality, but by His grace, the Lord allowed me to continue this labor of love.

On June 10, 2017, at Rock Church in Franklin, Virginia, I led our congregation in worship to "The Joy of the Lord." It was a powerful moment in our church. I could feel the Spirit moving through me. This wasn't anything I had done; it was a gift from the Father. Meanwhile, my husband of thirteen years, Ben, sat in the sound booth in the back of the church—recording me while I sang this new song I'd received, sharing this beautiful moment, this beautiful gift from God, with me.

Only God knew that, two days later, I'd wake up to find Ben dead on the floor of our shower.

The night before, my husband was in good health, only forty-three years old. We'd just finished a weekend full of family, friends, and celebration.

That morning, he was gone. Victim of a massive heart attack. The "widowmaker."

But that wasn't the end of the story. God had been preparing my heart for that moment. He knew what was coming, and He'd already given me my fight song:

> *For the Joy of the Lord*
> *Renews my strength*
> *The Joy of the Lord,*
> *The Joy of the Lord is my strength*

I should've been drowning in grief and loss, but all I could see was the hand of the Lord protecting me. All I could hear was His voice. All I could feel was a desire to worship and pray like never before.

> *I look to You for help*
> *For the pressures of life*
> *Bear down on me*

On that Monday—June 12, 2017—we started contending for Ben's resurrection story. Even in the midst of the grief, we praised God. As a congregation, God compelled us to go to the altar and pour ourselves out to Him. To surrender anything and everything. I could feel the level of faith rising—not only in our congregation, but also in me. Each day, I woke up with a new assignment from God:

> *Day 1: Hope*
> *Day 2: Persistence*
> *Day 3: Authority*
> *Day 4: Love*

I felt *alive*, in what felt like the truest sense of the word. In the most unexpected of times and ways, I experienced God's love and presence pouring out of me.

That Friday, more than *eight hundred people* showed up from all over the country to honor Ben's life. We filled up a dairy barn with worship and prayer. It looked like Noah's ark—people packed shoulder to shoulder, overflowing out the sides, cars backed up all the way down the road.

We started the funeral service by asking the Lord, one more time, to bring Ben back. I knew in my heart that it wasn't my call—it was the Father's—but boy, did we pray. And sing. And listen to the Holy Spirit. In front of all Ben's friends and family, I sang "The Joy of the Lord" again:

> *So let Your presence come*
> *And blow through me*
> *Let Your presence come*
> *'Til I am free*

We finished the service and headed to the gravesite. At the end of the day, Ben didn't wake up. But we, as a church body, absolutely did.

God gave me a revelation during that time: *presence trumps person*. Even before we finished praying for Ben's resurrection, I knew I was coming out the other side as a winner. This was my

"Job moment." Whatever happened, the name of the Lord would be praised. Whether Ben rose from the dead or not, I knew I'd awoken to God's presence in a new way. Out of that longing to be with Ben again, the Father gave me a renewed desire for His presence, for eternity.

This eternal philosophy started to become my way of life. In the wake of Ben's death, I had a new perspective. God-centered faith replaced man-centered faith. Instead of loss, I began to see through eyes of love. Even in the grief, I felt His nearness and comfort. Instead of running away from God, I began to run toward Him. That started me on this journey of discovering the Father's heart.

This album, *Heart Scribe Vibes*, came out of this loss. From that place of grief and pain and rawness, God began a new work in me, and these twelve songs are a result of that work. They're a transcription of the journey, my best attempt to communicate with you this gift God has given me. I picked up my pen, looked into my heart, and transcribed what I saw.

This book is meant to be a feast. As you consume these chapters, my hope is that they not only nourish your mind, but also your body and spirit. Like a good bone broth, you may need to let these words simmer and soak to draw out all the nutrients. I pray you feel His saturating presence on every page, as it has brought continuous healing to *my* mind, body, and spirit.

Each chapter allows you to take a bite inside the origin story of each song I uncovered—the context, what I was learning at the time, and what I learned *after*, as a result of the songwriting adventure. Each of these songs was inspired by the Divine while walking with Him in the mundane journey of life. In this process of creating new things, I've found that my heart has been speaking. Heart scribing is how I communicate with the Father. I hope my story will inspire you to also be a sensitive vessel to the words hidden within and to allow the Lord to use you as His scribe of Truth.

My prayer is that you enjoy a little bit of our dialogue—and that you'll do the same, in your own unique way. I believe God sent me these words to reverberate through the airwaves and find the ears that are searching for Truth wrapped in a melody. This is about becoming free, about discovering the Truth and letting it sink down into the depths of your heart. Yahweh is waiting to spend time with you. Will you let Him in?

When you give your time to seeking the Divine, there's a meal to be had—a *feast*. With Yahweh, you always walk away full. He'll never tell you to stop eating and there's always leftovers. Now, that's my kind of meal! Jesus eats with everyone. At His table, there's room enough for all of us. So come. Take a seat and *Bon appétit*.

A GUIDE TO SCRIBING AND VIBING:

1. Read each chapter with awareness.
2. Listen to the prayer at the end and meditate on the words.
3. Listen to each song and follow along with the lyrics.
4. Sit and soak. Don't move forward until you feel you've absorbed all that Yahweh wants to reveal and release through You.
5. And finally, scribe what your heart is vibing on the journal pages.

CHAPTER 1
HEART BEATS

Standing in the shower one morning—a place the enemy knew I'd be vulnerable to attack—a thought hit me out of the blue.

You didn't care.

In the last living memory of my husband, Ben, he came into our bedroom and told me his chest hurt. He seemed somewhat distressed, but we'd just had a full weekend of long nights and social interaction for a church convention. We didn't go to bed together until 1:30 a.m. that night, and I had nothing left. I'm not usually someone who gets tired easily.

"Can you pray for my chest?" Ben had asked.

"Sure," I had said.

After a quick prayer, I rolled over and fell back asleep. Everything seemed ordinary—we prayed together often for things like this—until it wasn't. I never imagined what I'd find when I got up that morning.

My husband of thirteen years, unconscious on the floor of the shower.

Frantically searching for my phone to dial 911.

The blur of the ambulance ride and flurry of doctors.

One of the nurses pulling me aside.

"I'm sorry for your loss."

Ben was gone.

You didn't care. You just rolled over like it was nothing.

My mind took me back to the Garden of Gethsemane, to Jesus's disciples falling asleep while He desperately pleaded with the Father:

> *"Later, he came back to his three disciples and found them all sound asleep. He awakened Peter and said to him,* **'Could you not stay awake with me for even one hour?'"** *(Matthew 26:40, TPT, bold emphasis mine)*

Could you not even stay awake with Ben for even one hour, Micah?

The accuser pulled out the big guns to target my character. To attack my identity.

You didn't do enough. You did nothing because you didn't care.

The devil was trying to plant something in me—the beat of a lie.

On top of our physical heartbeat, every one of us has another beat pulsating inside us. We all have different voices running through our minds. Occasional intrusive thoughts turn into repeated messages. Repeated messages become internal narratives. Internal narratives redefine our identities.

I am broken.

I am dirty.

I am worthless.

I am not enough.

These underlying narratives—stemming from past trauma, mistakes, and insecurity—beat us down, hour by hour, day by day. When we give in to the lies of the accuser, we begin to lose sight of the Creator. Our true identities get distorted. We can no longer see ourselves how God sees us. When we accept lies as truth, like Adam and Eve, we eat the forbidden fruit. Instead of regeneration through the Holy Spirit, we begin a process of *de*generation.

"

UNTIL WE
SURRENDER OURSELVES—
ALL OF OURSELVES—TO
THE FATHER OF LIGHT AND
ALLOW HIM TO WORK IN
US AGAIN, WE WON'T FIND
FREEDOM.

When we're insecure in our identity, the enemy successfully robs us. He robs us of the true identity Yahweh has given us as His children and replaces it with a false identity of shame.

"Oh my gosh!" we think. "This is who I am. *I'm not enough.*"

The more we listen and start to believe the enemy's lies within our minds, the more we want to hide. Because of the shame these false identities create, we start digging holes in our souls, sinking deeper into the darkness. We stop letting in the Father of Light. We build for ourselves *silent prisons*.

Because of the shame and the lies, we hide our true selves from others. We push down our doubts and insecurities. Our shame prevents us from talking about what's underneath the surface. And when we don't let any light *into* our souls, we can't let any *out*, either.

Too often in conversations, all we manage to say to the person next to us is, "I hope you had a good week!" There's something real off for me about that. How can we be friends with people—people we've done life with for years—and have no idea what's still beating them down? How can I claim to love my neighbors if I don't know what internal doubts are causing them to struggle?

When people have crises of faith, and their feelings are very raw, most cannot handle it. Their doubts trigger *our* internal doubts, and because we want to keep those hidden, we keep everyone at a distance. We don't like to be exposed. We don't like to ask ourselves, "Well, what if this happened to me?"

When we're insecure in our *own* identities—because of the beats of lies within our own minds—we can't be there for others.

When given the choice between facing our greatest fears or avoiding them, most of us choose our silent prisons.

Something's not right with that. That's an injustice to me.

Freedom comes in surrender. 1 Peter 5:7 (TPT) says, "Pour out all your worries and stress upon him and leave them there, for he always tenderly cares for you." Until we surrender ourselves—all of ourselves—to the Father of Light and allow Him to work in us again, we won't find freedom. We won't find healing. Healing doesn't come from hiding, self-preservation, or trying to control everything around us. Healing comes from letting go, from *allowing* Yahweh to start the process in us.

It's not selfish to practice self-care. That's a lie straight from the accuser himself. You're not self-absorbed if you focus on your own healing. If we don't take care of ourselves, we can't take care of others. Before we can support others in their doubts and struggles, we need to flush the pain out of our own bodies, minds, and souls. Not only does self-care say, "I care about myself, my body, and my mental health enough to steward it for the glory of God," it also says, "I care about *you* enough to take care of myself so I can be there for *you*."

When healing starts, we can't give the enemy any space to replant those beats of lies. Especially early on—in the times when we're most vulnerable—we need to have the Truth leading our brain cells. Whether it's Scripture, worship music, or encouragement from friends and family, we need to *fill our minds* with the Good and the True so *no space* remains for the enemy to penetrate the depth of us.

When I put worship music on in our house around my kids, it's so much better than the alternative. It pushes out the funky vibe. So often—and I know it's cliché—we fill our minds with garbage, with lies straight from the enemy. We listen to lyrics full of darkness. We play video games filled with violence and self-indulgence. That's what we're putting in the pantries of our souls. That's what we're planting in our hearts. It might be a catchy beat, but the lyrics are based on counterfeit belief. It's self-sabotage—and that's the enemy's slickest game.

Our own voices affect our minds and bodies more than any other voice. Your voice, your tone, your vibration can be your destroyer or your healer—depending on which voices you choose

"

WE NEED TO FILL OUR
MINDS WITH THE GOOD
AND THE TRUE, SO NO
SPACE REMAINS FOR THE
ENEMY TO PENETRATE THE
DEPTH OF US.

to amplify. The Word of God is our weapon—the "sword of the Spirit." When we speak words of truth to ourselves through Scripture, we deposit nourishing fruit within our souls. Yahweh has given us everything we need, y'all. We just need to believe it.

The more you say it, the more your mind believes it. The more you believe it, the more you start to see it. This takes work and effort and intentionality. It's that repetition—resetting the beat in our hearts. Over and over and over. The more you ingest the Good and the True, the more you invest in a rhythm of rest. When you find your pace, you will find His grace. Grace sustains when the pace remains. That faith is an activation.

Justin and Abi Stumvoll, in their class, "Living Fully Alive," say it like this:

> *"When you get a revelation of something within your heart, don't think it can instantly become your life. When the truth comes into your heart, it's an acquaintance. You've got to build a relationship with it. Usually, it takes about four years for that truth to be fully embodied."*

If you're early in the process and haven't seen much progress, don't be discouraged. Resetting your heartbeat takes time. It doesn't (always) happen overnight, but Yahweh is faithful. When we let Him in and allow Him to plant new truths in the gardens of our hearts, He transforms us from glory to glory. Intimacy doesn't just happen. That's not natural. Intimacy is a daily walk—gradually continuing to speak the Father's Truth over our lies and allowing Him to strip away every layer that's not from Him.

In this healing, we step out of the past and into the present. The past is a distortion. We cannot live there. It's not where we're supposed to live.

When Ben died, I needed to accept that he was gone. I couldn't focus only on what I'd lost; I needed to also focus on who I still had left. I had to fight to stay present, to break through the grief sitting inside me. For the sake of my kids and myself, I needed to step out of the past and into the reality in front of me. Stone and Stella had just lost Daddy—they couldn't lose Mommy, too.

When you're not present, you're living somewhere else. You're living outside God's plan for you. If you ruminate on the past, that's depression. It's focusing on the loss. If you ruminate on the future, that's anxiety. It's worrying about what you *might not have* instead of being content with what you do have. Those are not Kingdom emotions.

Cast all your cares on Him. We're not God. We need to step down from this God complex, this belief that we could've fixed everything in the past or we can fix everything in the future. We are not that big. We need to *trust* Yahweh. We need to listen to the *Father's* voice.

Since Ben's passing, the goal of my whole journey of discovering and understanding the Father's heart is to help me answer one key question: "Who said that?"

What's the pulse beating inside of me? Where is it coming from? Is it a lie from the accuser? Or is it Truth from the Father?

When we recognize the Father's voice and choose to listen to it, we find healing. We find security. We find protection from the enemy's attacks.

> *No beat of a lie*
> *Can deafen the Son*
> *I am who I am*
> *And I won't let go*

My desire is for my heart to beat with His heartbeat. That's my hope. That's my prayer and my cry—that our individual rhythms will align with the rhythms of the Father. Like Adam and Eve before the Fall, walking in the cool of the day with Yahweh, the goal is to walk in step with our Creator. This has been *His* desire for us since the beginning.

PRAYER

DEAR JESUS, HELP ME TO DISCERN YOUR VOICE MORE THAN WHEN THE ACCUSER'S VOICE IS SPEAKING TO ME. LET MY HEARTBEAT'S RHYTHM ALIGN WITH YOURS. AMEN.

 SCAN THE QR CODE TO HEAR MY SPECIAL PRAYER OVER YOU & LISTEN TO HEART BEATS (SENDINGANDMENDING.COM/HEART-BEATS)

Heart Beat Lyrics

No beat of a lie
Can deafen the Son
I know who I am
And I won't let go
Of my identity and how You see me
I am redeemed

No beat of a lie
Can deafen the Son
I know Whose I am
And I won't let, gooo oooh oooh oooh

I see You hanging there upon that cross
Broken and bruise but never lost

No beat of a lie
Can deafen the Son
I know Whose I am
And I won't let

I see You laying there inside that tomb
But soon for me there'll be an empty room
No beat of a lie
Can deafen the Son
I know Whose I am

And I won't let, gooo oooh oooh oooh
Gooo Oooh Oooh Oooh

'Cause my heart beats because of You
My heart only beats for You

I see You rising to eternity
And I know one day You'll be bringing me

No beat of a lie
Can deafen the Son
I know Whose I am
And I won't let

Now I know what You have done for me
I am redeemed for have You set me free

No beat of a lie
Can deafen the Son
I know Whose I am
And I won't let, gooo oooh oooh oooh

Gooo Oooh Oooh Oooh

'Cause my heart beats because of You
My heart only beats for You
(x2)

HEART SCRIBE JOURNAL

_____
_____
_____
_____
_____
_____
_____
_____
_____
_____
_____
_____
_____
_____
_____
_____
_____
_____
_____
_____

CHAPTER II
YOUR LOVING-KINDNESS

There was something about the energy of Jesus. I know "energy" is a word most of us don't like to use in the Western world—so use "magnetism," "vibes" or whatever suitable replacement fits best—but the positive, uplifting vibes Jesus gave off are undeniable in every account of Jesus's life.

When reading through the four Gospels, I always wondered, "How did all these people *find* Jesus?" In an era without the internet, without cell phones, Jesus followed the Father's compass into the most remote, secluded parts of the Ancient Near East—never in a rush, never with a strict agenda—yet, somehow, everyone seemed to find Him. It's like they sensed Him. They felt the positive energy He created. He could be in the middle of nowhere—on top of a mountain, even—and, as Matthew recounted, "massive crowds began following Him" (Matthew 8:1).

His magnitude drew the multitudes.

On one spring day in Virginia, everything was blooming. The azaleas, the dogwoods, the bluebells. Everything was lush. Everything was pretty. Everything was *full of life*. Wherever I looked, I became overwhelmed with all the goodness and beauty that surrounded me. It drew me in. That's when a lyric came to me:

Your loving-kindness is all around us
Through every battle, you're still in control

In that season, I'd fought many battles—battles most of us face daily—but in the process, I'd stopped looking around. I'd stopped listening. I'd stopped recognizing the evidence of God's goodness, mercy, and love that *literally* surrounded me every single day. I'd become so caught up in my own stuff, so self-absorbed with my own problems, that I'd missed the beauty. I'd missed that positive, magnetic energy of God. I'd missed the rainbow.

Later that summer, following the murder of George Floyd in Minneapolis, those battles many people in my city had battled for years began to rise to the surface—and quickly. In Virginia, across the United States, and around the world, the pain, hurt, and frustration of millions of people boiled over in a universal cry for justice. People wept and screamed. Cities burned. Business owners lost everything. Years and years of lost battles uncovered the true brokenness, darkness, and pain in every corner of our world.

In an already divisive time—in the middle of the COVID-19 pandemic—people became even more wary of each other. Suddenly, brothers and sisters divided against each other—by race, by ethnicity, by creed, by economic status. In the deep, stinging pain of another Black person dying without a voice, injustice drew lines between anyone and everyone.

That's when God told me a story.

From Genesis 18, in The Passion Translation (TPT), the section is called, "Abraham, the Intercessor":

"Afterward, the three men departed and walked toward

Sodom, and Abraham went off with them to see them on their way. As they walked, Yahweh said, 'Should I really hide from Abraham what I intend to do? After all, he will become a great and powerful nation, and every nation on earth will be blessed through him. It is true; I have singled him out as my own, so that he will lead his family and household to follow my ways and live by what is right and just. I will fulfill all the promises that I have spoken to him.'

Yahweh explained to Abraham, 'The outcry for justice against Sodom and Gomorrah is so great and their sins so blatant that I must go down and see if their wicked actions are as great as the outrage that has come to me, and if not, then I will know.'" (Genesis 18:16-21)

I don't know about you, but this story makes me feel some sort of way. Reading about Sodom and Gomorrah, I saw *my* city. I saw *my* community, my country. The darkness, brokenness, and sin of Sodom and Gomorrah caused people to cry out for justice. These people suffering under the abuses of those in power needed help, so they screamed out in pain. They needed answers, so they cried out for vengeance. They sought a solution of destruction.

But before Yahweh responded—before He moved forward with His plan—He stopped.

"As Yahweh's two companions went on toward Sodom, Abraham remained there, as Yahweh paused before Abraham." (Genesis 18:22)

I love this. Before Yahweh acts, before He gives the people what they're asking for, He pauses. He waits for Abraham. Even when judgment is imminent, Yahweh gives Abraham time to intercede.

"

YAHWEH IS NOT JUST A
GOD OF JUDGMENT. HE'S A
GOD OF MERCY AND LOVE.

And Abe steps up to the plate.

> *"So Abraham came forward to present his case before Yahweh, and said, 'Are you really going to sweep away the righteous while you judge the wicked? What if you find fifty righteous people in Sodom? Isn't your mercy great enough to forgive? Why judge the entire city at the cost of the fifty righteous who live there? **That's not who you are**—one who would slay the righteous with the wicked—treating them both the same way! Wouldn't the Merciful Judge of all the earth always do what is right?'"* (Genesis 18:23-25, bold emphasis mine)

Abraham doesn't try to convince Yahweh of the goodness of the people of Sodom. The character of the *people* was not what was on the line—it was the character of *God*.

"*That's not who you are.*"

So many people know Yahweh only as the "God of Judgment," the fire and brimstone. Our culture has created a domineering, heartless caricature of God that says, "Follow my rules, or else you will be punished." You don't hear about God's love. You don't hear about His mercy or His kindness. Of course, there are plenty of people who talk about God's goodness, but far too often, our world focuses on the judgment, the punishment, the condemnation.

But look at this story! Before Yahweh moves on to destroy Sodom and Gomorrah, He *pauses*! He *wants* Abraham to intercede for the people of Sodom. He *wants* Abraham to appeal to His mercy. It's as if, like Jesus said to Peter in Matthew 16:15, Yahweh asked Abraham, "Who do you say that I am?"

And Abraham responds, "That's *not* who you are."

For a girl who was questioning who He is, this was a key. This was a treasure I found in this chapter. "That's not who you are."

It's strong. "Isn't your mercy great enough to forgive?"

"And Yahweh said, 'Alright, if I find fifty righteous in Sodom, I will spare the whole city for their sake.'

Abraham spoke up again and said, 'I am just a man formed from earth's dust and ashes but allow me to be so bold as to ask you, my Lord. What if there are only five lacking and you only find forty-five righteous in Sodom? It's not who you are to destroy the entire city for lack of five righteous people.'

And Yahweh said, 'Alright, if I find forty-five righteous in Sodom, I will spare the whole city.'

'But what if there are only forty?' Abraham asked further. Yahweh answered, 'Alright. If I only find forty, I will spare the city.'

Abraham paused—then He said, 'Lord, please don't be offended with me, and let me speak…What if there are only thirty?'

Yahweh answered, 'Alright. If I find only thirty, I will spare the city.'

Abraham ventured even further, asking, 'Allow me to dare speak this way to you, my Lord. But what if you find there only 20 righteous?'

Yahweh answered, 'Alright, for the sake of the twenty, I will not destroy the city.'

*Then Abraham took a deep breath and asked, 'Once more,
please don't let my Lord be angry with me if I make but
one more request. What if you find only ten righteous?'*

*And Yahweh answered, 'Alright, I will extend my mercy
and not destroy the city for the sake of ten righteous.'*

*Yahweh finished speaking with Abraham. He immediately
went on his way, and Abraham returned home."*
(Genesis 18:26-33)

The footnote in the TPT says, "Abraham appeals to Yahweh,
not only to spare the righteous, but for his merciful heart to be
expressed...Abraham stands alone before Yahweh and pleads for
the lives of the wicked people to be spared. This moved God's
heart, and He granted each request Abraham made until Abraham
stopped asking. Abraham asked six times. What would have
happened if Abraham had asked a seventh time? Abraham did not
change the mind of God. He demonstrated what was already on
God's heart."

Abraham came into alignment with the heart of God. Yahweh
paused, and Abraham came through as an intercessor for the
people of Sodom. He pleaded for justice for the righteous and
mercy for the wicked. "What would have happened if Abraham
had asked a seventh time?" How far would God's mercy have
extended?

After reading that chapter—amid everything going on—I went
out to my porch. As I listened to the chants from the protests near
my home, the Spirit told me to pray, to intercede for these people
experiencing injustice.

"Lord, who's standing watch over my city? Who is the watchman?
Who are the intercessors? Are you calling us to be the intercessors?
Am I that one who's supposed to intercede for our city? How

far will Your mercy, Your grace, Your loving-kindness extend to transform my community?"

That's when I came back to the lyric that came to me earlier that spring:

> *Your loving-kindness is all around us*
> *Through every battle, you're still in control*

Who are the intercessors for our cities, our communities, our people? Who will stand in the gap when we hear cries for justice? Who will be the one to say, "No, I know the character of God. This is *not* who You are." Who will appeal to Yahweh and say, "As for this city, can you show Your mercy?"

He's waiting for us. He's pausing. He's lingering for us to appeal to His good character, to His mercy, to His loving-kindness. Yahweh is not just a God of judgment. He's a God of mercy and love. He wants us to stand in the gap, to cry out to Him on behalf of others, on behalf of the brokenness in our cities. He wants us to appeal to His good character. He is a God who always gives, not one who only takes away.

Despite the eventual destruction of Sodom and Gomorrah, Genesis 18 brings us *good news.* It's a good news story! It shows us that God *wants* us to intercede for others, for our neighborhoods, for our world. He *wants* us to appeal to His good character, to His loving-kindness—the same loving-kindness so evident all around us.

Through creation, the Father sends us His energy, His positive vibes. In the blooming flowers of spring and the soft snowfall of winter, Yahweh shows us His good character. As Jesus's magnitude drew the multitudes, so the Father draws His creation to Him through His loving-kindness. It's all around us. We just need to slow down enough to see it.

And it's not just in nature, in the azaleas and the dogwoods.

It can't stop there. We need to see the goodness in *each other*. If we want to see unity in our world, we *need* to see God's loving-kindness in ourselves, in others. We *need* to appeal to God's mercy, love, and grace. We have a choice—a choice of perspective. We can see the hurt and the pain—we can see ourselves always as the victims—or we can look around and see the azaleas. We can tune in to the noise of the world, or we can listen to the voice of the Father.

His loving-kindness is all around us. Through every battle, He's in control. Will you make the choice to see it? To recognize it? To stop and embrace it?

I see goodness. I hope you do, too.

PRAYER

DEAR JESUS, OPEN MY EYES TO SEE THE NEEDS OF THOSE AROUND ME AND NOT BE CONSUMED BY MY OWN PROBLEMS. HELP ME TO SEE YOUR LOVINGKINDNESS AND GOODNESS ALL AROUND ME. AMEN.

 SCAN THE QR CODE TO HEAR MY SPECIAL PRAYER OVER YOU & LISTEN TO YOUR LOVING KINDNESS (SENDINGANDMENDING.COM/YOUR-LOVING-KINDNESS)

Your Loving-Kindness Lyrics

I see Your kindness
All over Your face
I cry out for mercy
Over my city

Send forth Your mercy
Through the power of grace
Send forth Your mercy
Over my city

Cause, Your loving-kindness
Is all around us
Through every battle
You're still in control

And, I see Your kindness
Transforming this place
With every heartbeat
You radiate

We see Your kindness
All over this place
May Your power and grace
Keep transforming this place

Cause, Your loving-kindness
Is all around us
Through every battle
You're still in control

Through every battle
Through every battle
Through every battle
You're still in control

Cause, it's Your transforming grace
That shines through our face
(x4)

Send forth Your mercy
Through the power of grace
Send forth Your mercy
Over my city

Cause, Your loving-kindness
Is all around us
Through every battle
You're still in control

Your loving-kindness
Is all around us
Through every battle
You're still in control

HEART SCRIBE JOURNAL

CHAPTER III
DAUGHTER OF THE KING

In the summer of 2017, every place in which I found my identity started crumbling beneath my feet. In June, Ben's death shattered the identity I'd formed as a wife. In my newfound role of single mother to our two kids, Stone and Stella, I put my identity as a real estate agent on hold.

To add insult to injury, by the fall, I'd almost completely lost my voice. When I went to the doctor for a diagnosis, they found nodules on both of my vocal cords.

I was no longer a wife.

No longer a real estate agent.

No longer a singer or worship leader.

In my desperation and confusion, I began to ask God, "Who do You say that I am?"

After months of seeking, praying, and asking questions, I attended a worship night with my sister-in-law and pastor, Jill Dillon. Kari Jobe, one of my all-time favorite artists, performed the song, "No Longer Slaves," by Bethel Music, Jonathan David and Melissa Helser:

> *I'm no longer a slave to fear*
> *I am a child of God*

As Kari's words from the chorus washed over us, Jill turned to me. She knew—maybe more than anyone—what I'd experienced during those past few months. She knew my pain, my identity struggle. She knew how hard I'd been praying.

"Micah," she said. "You are a child of God!"

For someone else, that might have been a simple or obvious connection, but for me, it hit me like a ton of bricks. It was like a bomb went off on my insides. I just broke—but something was also implanted inside of me.

That's it. I'm a God-girl. I'm a daughter of the King.

That song from Bethel finds its origin from Paul's words in Galatians 4:

> *"Let me illustrate: As long as an heir is a minor, he's not really much different than a servant, although he's the master over all of them. For until the time appointed by the father, the child is under the domestic supervision of the guardians of the estate. So it is with us. When we were juveniles we were enslaved under the hostile spirits of the world. But when the time of fulfillment had come, God sent his Son, born of a woman, born under the law. Yet all of this was so that he would redeem and set free those held hostage to the law so that we would receive our freedom and a full legal adoption as his children. And so that we would know that we are his true children, God released the Spirit of Sonship into our hearts—moving us to cry out intimately, 'My Father! My true Father!' Now we're no longer living like slaves under the law, but we enjoy being God's very own sons and daughters! And because we're his, we can access everything our Father has—for we are heirs because of what God has done!"*
> *(Galatians 4:1–7, TPT)*

The truth finally began to take root in my soul. God wasn't looking for me to become a more award-winning real estate agent—or even a more compelling worship leader. Those things don't connect Him to my heart. If I'm not singing, selling houses, and raising my kids with a right understanding of my identity, then I'm missing the mark. God has given me a Spirit of Sonship! I needed to shift from man-centered faith to God-centered faith.

Before I established my identity in anything else, I needed to first understand my identity as a child of God. I needed to go on a journey of discovering the Father's heart.

Who is He?

What is He like?

What does He think of me?

If my true identity came from my inherent worth and value as a child of God, then what did that mean?

Again, I started asking God, "Who is a daughter of the King?"

During the course of several months, across a variety of different encounters, conversations, and experiences, the Holy Spirit put five words on my heart—five defining characteristics of a "Daughter of the King":

1. **Righteous**
2. **Royal**
3. **Regal**
4. **Real**
5. **Raw**

Righteous means someone in right relationship with God—not because of anything they've done, but because of Christ's work on the cross. *Royal* means "kingly," elevated to the role of High Priest. *Regal* means someone so impressive, beautiful, and dignified that they're suitable to be a king or a queen. *Raw* exemplifies pure

"

WHEN WE RECOGNIZE WHO
WE ARE—ROYAL, REGAL,
RIGHTEOUS CHILDREN
OF THE KING—AND THE
WEIGHT THAT HOLDS,
WE CARRY THE NAME
OF JESUS WITH A NEW
REVERENCE.

transparency and vulnerability, uninfluenced by the eyes of public opinion. *Real* reflects honesty and authenticity, living in line with one's genuine self.

Wow, I remember thinking at the time. *I like that!*

In my mind, these five traits break down into two groups.

First, *righteous*, *royal*, and *regal*. All three of those characteristics have to do with *knowing* our identity as children of God. It's recognizing the power that lives within us and learning to walk and embody those things. Like Esther, Ruth, Miriam, Deborah, Hannah, and all the other courageous women of the Bible, a Daughter of the King knows her true identity as a Daughter of *Light*.

I wrote in my journal something I felt the Holy Spirit gave me during that period of searching and asking questions. Eventually, part of that writing turned into another song on this album ("Rays"):

> *"So, Daughters of Light, it's time to carry his might. Step outside and look into the light, for we are walking by faith and not by sight. Because we are Daughters of Light, and we carry His might. For this is the choice to raise our voice with the weight of God's glory."*

In a class I took on studying the Bible through a Middle Eastern lens, I learned about the phrase, "taking the Lord's name in vain." Like many people, I always thought that meant, "Don't cuss" or "Don't say, 'Oh my God,'" but as I learned in this class, that's not all the biblical author is trying to convey.

As followers of Jesus, as Christians (or "little Christs"), we represent Jesus to the world. As sons and daughters of Yahweh, we stand in on behalf of our Father of Light to the people around us. But if we don't know who we are—if we don't understand our identity—our representation holds no weight. We carry the name of Jesus, but without all the glory, honor, and righteousness it deserves. This is what it means to "take the Lord's name in vain."

When we recognize who we are—*royal*, *regal*, *righteous* children of the King—and the weight that holds, we carry the name of Jesus with a new reverence. Like the "glory dust" I refer to in this song—the "loving-kindness" that's all around us—a Daughter of the King wears a garment of glory that's characteristic of her Father. It carries weight. This is how Yahweh views us as His children—our words carry weight.

Then there's the flipside to this identity as a child of God. Not only is she *righteous*, *royal*, and *regal*—knowing her identity as Yahweh's child—she's also *raw* and *real*.

There's an interesting dichotomy to that. It's not too often you connect the words *royal* and *regal* with *raw* and *real*. Typically, royalty comes with a sense of distance and self-preservation, not authenticity and vulnerability. People don't think of the Queen of England as "raw and real." But that's what separates a Daughter of the King from the rest of the world. Not only does she know who she is and *whose* she is; she also isn't ashamed of any part of herself. She doesn't need to hide or put on a mask because she's ashamed of what's underneath the surface. A Daughter of the King isn't worried about the *external*, about what other people think. She walks with finesse and grace, confident enough in the *internal* to be authentic and vulnerable, to be fully raw and real.

When I was a kid—I don't remember this, but my mom told me later—I used to change clothes *all the time*. Two or three times a day (at least), I'd dig through my little wardrobe—because we lived in an old farmhouse, we didn't have closets—and pick out a new outfit. My life was so focused on the external, on trying to earn other people's validation through how I looked. If people approved of the outside of my life, I thought, maybe everything on the inside was all right.

I looked pretty on the outside, but inside, I wasn't that great.

The external earned priority over the internal, and as a result, the internal suffered. Most of the emotions I internalized growing up were negative—fear, disappointment, shame, even embarrassment. Because I couldn't handle all the emotions at once, living in a house of five, I learned to tune out or turn them off. That was my coping mechanism (as I learned later, this is called "disassociation"). I ran from my feelings. It didn't feel safe to sit with them. For *thirty-seven years*, I never understood how much shame I carried in my body. I just stuffed it all down and projected an image of myself to the world that made it look like I had it all together. I stopped taking risks. I stopped being my authentic self. I couldn't afford it. *What if people discovered who I really was?*

But God was still there. He was present with me and my parents the whole time. Even though I couldn't see Him—even though I focused on the outside-in instead of the inside-out—the Father still worked in my life. I didn't smoke or drink, but, as I realized later, I didn't do it for Jesus—I just didn't want to get fat or have wrinkles! But God still used it to protect me! Yahweh meets us where we are. He works with what He's got. More than that, *He never stops pursuing us.*

The Father of Light wasn't done with me. My shame and external projections didn't keep the Holy Spirit from invading my life. Jesus found me, and He gave me a new identity.

There is no place for shame within our story as God's children. Yahweh created you. He's the only One who fully knows you, yet still, He's the only One who truly, fully loves you. When we're raw and real, we not only uncover the righteous, royal, and regal children of God that we are; we also allow God to fully step into our lives and bring to light our true identities. This allows us to walk out of external, performance-based living and into His life-giving, transformational, grace-filled freedom. When we give Jesus our full selves—past shame and all—we allow Him to, as

Brooke Ligertwood of Hillsong Worship put it, make "new wine" out of us:

> *Make me Your vessel*
> *Make me an offering*
> *Make me whatever*
> *You want me to be*
> *I came here with nothing*
> *But all You have given me*
> *Jesus bring new wine out of me*

So, child of God, be ***regal***, ***royal***, and ***righteous***. It's who you are. You carry the weight of His glory dust. And be ***raw*** and ***real***. It's worth it. The Creator has a tender, healing hand—no matter what He reveals about your past. It hurts only for a moment.

> *Run wild and free, My child. Be who I created you to be.*
> *And when you call out to Me, I'll be right there. For your*
> *Heavenly Father is everywhere. You belong to Me, My*
> *child. You belong to Me.*

——— PRAYER ———

DEAR JESUS, I DESIRE TO BE REGAL, ROYAL, RIGHTEOUS, RAW AND REAL. THANK YOU FOR CREATING ME TO WALK IN YOUR TRUE IDENTITY. SHAME YOU HAVE NO HOLD ON ME FOR I AM FREE. AMEN.

 SCAN THE QR CODE TO HEAR MY SPECIAL PRAYER OVER YOU & LISTEN TO DAUGHTER OF THE KING (SENDINGANDMENDING.COM/DAUGHTER-OF-THE-KING)

Daughter of the King Lyrics

Shame has a way of trying to stay
Shame has to go down, down down his hole
Go down go down, back to the place
Go down go down, from which you came

There is no shame in my story
Only pain for His glory
There is no shame in my story, yeah

Cause, I'm a daughter of the king and I hope now
you see it
He's ruling and reigning inside me, yeah
(x2)

I don't feel shame to tell my story
I don't feel shame where I'm going
I see Your glory. It's before me
I see Your glory. It's all around me

There is no shame in my story
Only pain for His glory
There is no shame in my story, yeah

Cause, I'm a daughter of the king and I hope now
you see it
He's ruling and reigning inside me, yeah
(x2)

Bring Your glory dust
And cover all of us
All the glory
All the glory
(x2)

I said, Your glory dust is all around us
All the glory
All the glory

I said, Your glory dust is all around us, yeah

Cause, I'm a daughter of the king and I hope now
you see it
He's ruling and reigning inside me, yeah
(x2)

Shame has a way of trying to stay

HEART SCRIBE JOURNAL

_____
_____
_____
_____
_____
_____
_____
_____
_____
_____
_____
_____
_____
_____
_____
_____
_____
_____
_____
_____
_____

CHAPTER IV
TOKEN

From the sideline of Stone's soccer game, I texted a friend. She asked how Stone was playing. At that point in the game, though, he hadn't made it past the sideline.

"Well, he'll get to play only if they're up big," I texted back. "He's the token."

In my mind, Stone was the token young kid playing up with the higher-level traveling soccer team. The one who stood a head shorter than half the team, who'd only see game action in a complete blowout. The one who the crowd and rest of the team would cheer on to score—but only because the outcome of the game was already decided. Stone *earned* a spot on that team on merit—he was good enough to play with boys several years older than him—but on that day, because his team trailed by multiple goals, I knew he wasn't making it off the bench. So, my mind went to the negative: *If he's just the number on the back of the jersey, why are we even here?*

In my mind, Stone was a token. Because he didn't have any significant value, he stayed on the sideline.

Hold up.

I had to stop myself mid-thought, mid-text.

What am I saying?

My son doesn't have any value?

What label am I putting on my son, who has immense *value—not only to me and his family, but also to his Creator?*

I needed to straighten myself out.

No, Stone. Don't listen to me. You're not *a token. You're nobody's token.*

Sitting on the sideline with the other parents and families, that realization sparked something in me. When we got back home after the game, I pulled out my journal and asked the Holy Spirit what all of it meant.

"Can You share with me more about 'token'?" I wrote.

The response came in the next line.

"You get a token to ride a ride, to play a game. A token is a pawn, a means to an end."

That is *enemy language.*

Enemy language. In the eyes of the world, this is what so many of us—if not *all* of us—represent. We're tokens. Even the best of us are minimized to one-dimensional versions of ourselves by the world, other people, and—the one behind all of it—the devil. The enemy.

"Oh, that's Micah, the widow."

"That's Stone, the token."

"That's (fill in the blank), the singer/writer/overachiever/liar/drama queen/cheater/failure."

The enemy takes one part of us—most often, pain and brokenness from our past—and says, "This is who you are. You are a token. You're a means to an end. You're replaceable, a dime a dozen. You had one job, but you couldn't even do *that* right. You must be worthless."

How many of us think like this? How many of us fall into these lies the enemy puts in our heads, based on our past mistakes?

He wants to make it *personal.* He takes our past mistakes,

"

IN THAT SPACE OF
VULNERABILITY AND
BROKENNESS AND
MISALIGNED IDENTITY, THE
FATHER OF LIGHT REACHES
DOWN UNDERNEATH
OUR SHAME TO FILL US
WITH HIS LOVE AND LIFT
US BACK TO A PLACE OF
HONOR.

our trauma, our points of insecurity, and twists our minds into believing they *define* us. That *we are* the brokenness of our past. That *we are* our job loss, failed relationship, dead-end career, etc.

For me, it came after my church family and I fought for my husband's resurrection. After four days of praying, worshiping, and pleading with God to bring Ben back, only to be met with silence, the enemy tried to sneak a message into my brain:

You're not enough.

It was subtle, but extremely effective.

You weren't enough to bring back Ben. You didn't pray hard enough. You didn't have enough faith.

You're not enough.

That was a thought the accuser used to try to break me, to try to redefine my identity in brokenness and lies.

That's not all of it, though. It's only a *part* of the enemy's game plan. Not only does he want us to *personalize* our brokenness and shame; he also wants us to *internalize* it. In our own minds, he wants that message—"You're not enough"—to ring loud and clear, but to the outside world, he wants it hidden behind a veil. He wants us to stay in the darkness—alone, ashamed, helpless. He wants us isolated and living in fear.

Oh no, you can't share that. *What will people think? What will people say?*

You need to keep that to yourself.

I wasn't having *any* of that. Even thinking back on it, I felt some sort of way about it. I don't usually cuss, but this season had me ready to spray all sorts of verbal artillery back at the enemy.

Devil, get the freak *out of here.*

Who else could this be except for the father of lies? Who else would want to not only 1) cover us in shame and darkness but also 2) isolate us from the love of God and those around us? Who else would want to turn us into one-dimensional tokens, worthless pieces of metal for someone to throw away at will?

I'm not your token, devil.

That's where Yahweh meets us. In that space of vulnerability and brokenness and misaligned identity, the Father of Light reaches down underneath our shame to fill us with His love and lift us back to a place of honor. This is *justice*. In Him—and *only* in Him—we can change our relationship to our circumstances. Only in Christ can we change our identities from victims to empowered children of God.

The circumstances of a victim *define* them. A victim says, "My circumstances dictate who I am. If *you* didn't do that, *I* wouldn't have responded this way. *You* are the cause of my suffering."

I've experienced brokenness; therefore, I am broken.

But an empowered person changes the game. A Spirit-filled child of God takes satan's attack and turns it over, completely onto its head.

I may experience brokenness, but I'll never be broken.

An empowered person looks the devil in the eyes and says, "I see you. I see what you're trying to do. I see the brokenness of my past. But it doesn't matter. You can't take my peace because I have peace within. My peace is not circumstantial. I'm grounded. I'm stable. I'm being cemented in my faith."

Not only that, but when we're grounded in our identity and can see the enemy's attacks coming, we can flip the script. We can take what satan intends for evil and flip it for God's glory. We can lift our own brokenness to God for Him to use for a bigger purpose.

We all deal with this every day. We all ask ourselves, "Am I enough?" If we give in to satan and hide our past mistakes, hide our brokenness, we miss an opportunity. When we try to protect ourselves through isolation and reservation, we don't allow God to step in and use our weakness for good. But when we're authentic and vulnerable—about all parts of ourselves, good and bad—our weakness becomes a *portal for God's glory*.

Look at what Paul wrote about his "thorn in the flesh":

"

WHEN WE ARE WEAK, HE IS STRONG. BECAUSE OF YAHWEH'S LOVE FOR US, WE DON'T HAVE TO GIVE IN TO SHAME OR FEAR.

"The extraordinary level of the revelations I've received is no reason for anyone to exalt me. For this is why a thorn in my flesh was given to me, the Adversary's messenger sent to harass me, keeping me from becoming arrogant. Three times I pleaded with the Lord to relieve me of this. But he answered me, 'My grace is always more than enough for you, and my power finds its full expression through your weakness.' So I will celebrate my weaknesses, for when I'm weak I sense more deeply the mighty power of Christ living in me. So I'm not defeated by my weakness, but delighted! For when I feel my weakness and endure mistreatment—when I'm surrounded with troubles on every side and face persecution because of my love for Christ—I am made yet stronger. For my weakness becomes a portal to God's power."
(2 Corinthians 12:7–10, TPT, bold emphasis mine)

That's a flip! Paul is changing the game on the enemy.

"So I will *celebrate* my weaknesses, for when I'm weak, I sense more deeply the mighty power of Christ living in me."

When we are weak, He is strong. Because of Yahweh's love for us, we don't have to give in to shame or fear. I don't have to hide my past sins or mistakes. I don't have to stuff anything away for fear of other people rejecting me. His love is more than enough for me.

I'm working on a song about Peter walking on the water. The first verse starts like this:

I feel You drawing me into the sea
You tell me just to believe
So I keep my eyes on Thee
Oh, I feel the waves crashing over me

Too often, we look at the story of Peter walking on the water, and we think, "How could anybody do that? He took the risk. He stepped out onto the waves." But in doing so, we miss a *key* part of that passage: *what drew Peter out of the boat?* The bridge of the song goes like this:

> *Even through the raging sea*
> *Your love crashes over me*

It's His *love*. That's what drew Peter out of the boat and onto the sea: the magnitude of Jesus and wanting to be near to Him. Peter was drawn to his Father and his Friend. He wanted to be with Him. It's not the *fear* that's crashing over Peter; it's the love of Jesus.

Here's one more verse of the song:

> *I hear You say, "Just look at Me."*
> *Oh, I feel the waves crashing all over me*
> *I can't take my eyes off Thee*
> *Will You rescue me from the sea?*
> *For Your love crashes over me*
>
> *When I see You, I see the best in me*
> *You created me for intimacy*
> *Wait for me, for I'm walking toward Thee*
> *Because I know I can trust You'll hold me*
> *Your love crashes over me*

His loving-kindness is all around us, y'all! That's the flip! We need to stop telling the story from the *fear* perspective. What about the love? What about the love perspective? Can we get back to that? His love is all around us! It's more than enough for us! Bring on the wind and the waves, satan, because I'm holding onto Yahweh, the *Anchor*.

When faced with the world's perspective, we have a choice: we can take it and embrace it, or we can flip it. God doesn't see us as one-dimensional. We're not tokens to Yahweh. We're not a means to any ends for Him. We *are* His end game.

To God, You are *more than* a token. You're not broken. You're His creation. You are marked. You are enough. You are a *child of the King*.

Nice try, devil, but you can't break me down—no matter how hard you try. Your game of accusatory words only fuels my fire to fight harder. You forgot that I'm a child of the King, and I see your angle— finally. And yeah, there's some brokenness in here, but instead of you taking it and shaming me for it, I'm going to flip it for His glory. My weakness is a portal to God's power. I finally see it now. When I am weak, He is strong.

> I'm not your token.
> And I'll never be broken.
> Just you wait and see.

PRAYER

DEAR JESUS, THANK YOU THAT I AM ENOUGH. THANK YOU THAT I AM MORE THAN A TOKEN IN YOUR SIGHT, FOR I AM FOREVER A CHILD OF THE KING! AMEN.

 SCAN THE QR CODE TO HEAR MY SPECIAL PRAYER OVER YOU & LISTEN TO TOKEN (SENDINGANDMENDING.COM/TOKEN)

Token Lyrics

The world may say you are a token
The world may say you look broken
The world may say you are no keepsake
But, make no mistake, make no mistake

You are more than, more than a token
For God said you will never be broken
For He created more, more than
You're more than a token, you're more than a token

You may experience brokenness
But, you will never be broken
For He that is within is more than
Is more than

I'm not your token
And I'll never be broken
Just you wait and see, wait and see
(x2)

So, when you feel down and done
And you're overwhelmed and want to run
Know you were created for more than
You're more than a token, you're more than a token
So, when you feel like you're not enough
And you want to just give up

God said you are My child and you'll never be broken
For I marked you, marked you, marked you

Ouuu, Ouuu, Ouuuuu
(I'm not your token and I'll never be broken)

You will forever be a child of the King
You will forever be a child of the King, yeah
For, you will forever be a child of the King
You will forever be a child of the King, yeah
You will forever be a child of the King
A child of the King, yeah

Yes, the brokenness is the beautiful thing inside of me
Yes, the brokenness is the beautiful thing breaking out of me
Yes, the brokenness is the beautiful thing pouring
out of me, yeah
Just you wait and see, wait and see, wait and see

I'm not your token
And I'll never be broken
Just you wait and see, wait and see, wait and see

I'm not your token
And I'll never be broken
Just you wait and see, wait and see, wait and see

Just you wait and see, wait and see, wait and see
(x3)

HEART SCRIBE JOURNAL

_____
_____
_____
_____
_____
_____
_____
_____
_____
_____
_____
_____
_____
_____
_____
_____
_____
_____
_____
_____
_____

CHAPTER V

TREASURE HOLDER

"How do you treasure your treasure?"

It was a question Justin and Abi Stumvall, life coaches out of Redding, California, asked a small group of us at a virtual class called "Living Fully Alive." I was looking to gain language and Kingdom perspective on my emotions.

"Do you believe you're a treasure? How do you value yourself?"

As an activation exercise, they asked us to imagine we were holding a ball of light that represented our worth as a human being. They wanted us to uncover who *held* our worth—ourselves or someone (or some*thing*) else).

"Ask your heart, 'Who did I give this to?'"

For my niece, the answer came quickly and loudly. Almost instantly, faces began to appear in her mind. Mine didn't come for another two days.

Sitting at home, answering emails and texts from my real estate clients, I thought back to times when I sat at the closing table, talking through extra expenses that had come up during the home-buying process. On multiple occasions, my clients would turn to me and ask, "Can you cut some of your commission to make this work?"

There's a rule in real estate, especially when it comes to closing: "Some money is better than no money." So, plenty of times, when my clients asked me to take a cut, I did it. I wanted to close the deal. But almost every time, as I drove home after signing the papers, I felt bad about myself. To be completely honest, I felt worthless, like my clients had taken advantage of me. My services weren't rendered satisfactory, so my clients docked my pay. I wasn't worth their money.

That's when it hit me: I gave my ball of light to my money. My self-worth was tied to my *net* worth. Every day, I fought for my commission—that's how I perceived it. I had to fight off other people, other factors, and other situations to earn my commission, to find my treasure. If I didn't—or if I had to sacrifice some of that treasure along the way—I had less value as a human being.

It's the trap so many of us get caught in every day: we find our worth in our performance. Whether it's pleasing other people, having a certain job title, or earning a certain salary, it's all temporary. We may feel treasured when we *accomplish* what we treasure, but that's *still* performance-based living. We're still trapped in the sinking sand of temporary, earthly identities. We believe we're worth something only when we do something to *earn* that worth.

Jesus told a parable in Matthew 13—maybe you have heard it. In The Passion Translation (TPT), it goes like this:

> *"Heaven's kingdom realm can be illustrated like this: 'A person discovered that there was hidden treasure in a field. Upon finding it, he hid it again. Because of uncovering such treasure, he was overjoyed and sold all that he possessed to buy the entire field just so he could have the treasure. Heaven's kingdom realm is also like a jewel merchant in search of rare pearls. When he discovered one very precious and exquisite pearl, he immediately gave up*

all he had in exchange for it.'" (Matthew 13:44-46)

Like most people, I always understood that parable in one way. I am the person discovering the hidden treasure, which is Jesus. To follow Jesus and enter His Kingdom, I need to give up everything. It's a perfectly reasonable and understandable explanation. But then I saw a footnote in the TPT for verse 44. Here's what it says:

> *"The most accepted interpretation of this parable is that Jesus is the treasure, but Jesus taught that the field is the world (v. 38). The allegory breaks down, for a believer doesn't sell all he has (works) and then buy the world to find Jesus (the treasure). It is more plausible to view the* hidden treasure as a symbol of you and me. *Jesus is the man who sold all that he owned, leaving his exalted place of glory to come and pay for the sin of the whole world with his own blood just so he could have you, his treasure. Heaven's kingdom realm is experienced when we realize what a great price Jesus places on our souls, for he gave his sacred blood for us. The re-hiding of the treasure is a hint of our new life, hidden in God."*

You are the hidden treasure. You are the precious, exquisite pearl. Jesus gave up everything—He paid the ultimate sacrifice to find you. To find me.

I grew up in an old farmhouse from the mid-1800s with no storage and one bathroom that remained unfinished for half my life. When you live in a place like that—a home that always feels incomplete—it does something to you. For me, it created a scarcity mentality, this feeling of never having enough, never *being* enough.

My parents worked faithfully to provide for us—they were good stewards of what they were given, and I know God blessed their

"

THE CROSS GIVES US A
NEW IDENTITY. WE ARE
THE HIDDEN TREASURE,
THE EXQUISITE PEARL.

work—but still, money became a stronghold for me. Growing up, I often wished for a different life—one in which money was no object. I had a very independent spirit, and I believed I had to conquer to gain. So, at sixteen, I got a job, and the hustle became real. The taste of money was pleasing, and it set up an external, performance-based value system in my heart.

That system turned the key and controlled the dials of my life. I had to prove myself in my job. I had to earn a higher salary. I had to avoid that feeling of *not being enough*. And, for me, the only way I knew how to numb that internal voice was to *win the deal*.

The other day, I was singing the old song, "Here I Am to Worship," by Tim Hughes from the early 2000s. When I came across the bridge, I stopped:

> *I'll never know how much it cost*
> *To see my sin upon that cross.*

As I listened to it over and over, the Holy Spirit gave me another line:

For the cross crushed the shame of sin within.

The cross crushed the shame of sin within. Finally, it hit me— if we really understand the revelation of the cross, we realize its power over our sin and our shame. It *crushes* those things. The power of shame has no power over the cross. Because of the cross, my past of shame and scarcity doesn't have to be my story. Your past of addiction, trauma, abuse—that doesn't have to be your story. Because of Jesus, because of the cross, we've been set free.

The enemy wants you to believe otherwise. He wants to convince you to hide your shame, to hide your story—because if it comes out, it will *define* you. That's man-centered faith.

"There is no treasure in your story (of shame, of abuse, of

addiction, of generational sin, etc.)," the enemy says. "Keep it hidden. Numb the pain."

But that's not what Jesus says. The character of Yahweh is *incompatible* with shame. God-centered faith says:

> *"No, you are* not *defined by the events, the trauma, the relationships of your past. You—and your past—are defined by* Me *and* My love.*"

The cross gives us a new identity. We are the hidden treasure, the exquisite pearl. It's not man-centered. It's not performance-based. We did nothing to deserve it. I wasn't even a *thing* when Jesus died on the cross, yet I still have unlimited access to His favor, His mercy, His grace, kindness, and love. There's a phrase I heard used often in church retreats: "It was your sin that put Jesus on the cross, but it was *His love for you* that kept Him there." Jesus died on the cross to give us a new identity as His treasure. Jesus *stayed* on that cross because we *are* His treasure.

You were worth it. Regardless of your past, your sin, your shame, you were worth it for Jesus to die on the cross. You matter not because of what you've done, but because *you're here.* You're here now, fulfilling your purpose. You matter *now.*

So, back to that question from Justin and Abi: "How do you treasure your treasure?"

Matthew 6:21, in the NIV, says, "For where your treasure is, there your heart will be also." In the TPT, it says, "For your heart will always pursue what you esteem as your treasure."

What is *your treasure*? Where do you spend your time? What has become an idol in your life? Entertainment? Family? Social events? Video games? Scrolling on social media?

To whom do you give your worth?

For so long, my treasure came out of a reaction to my past. I ran from my childhood by pursuing the treasure of money. I built up earthly treasures instead of treasures in heaven. Look at the next two verses in Matthew 6—again, in the TPT:

> *"The eyes of your spirit allow revelation-light to enter into your being. If your heart is unclouded, the light floods in! But if your eyes are focused on money, the light cannot penetrate and darkness takes its place. How profound will be the darkness within you if the light of truth cannot enter!" (Matthew 6:22–23)*

God is a gardener. He's planted His goodness, His light, His Spirit deep within the recesses of our hearts—and He wants to continue to plant things. But until we're ready to dig deep, until we're courageous enough to cut into the darkness of our sin, shame, and past to expose that darkness to the light, those seeds will never germinate. They can't survive in the darkness. They need the revelation-light of the Son! If we continue to trade our true treasure for temporary pleasures, we'll never see true growth. By numbing the pain, we're suffocating what God wants to do in us through His love.

That's what this song is—it's a reflection of two truths that came to me: 1) God actually sees me as His hidden treasure, and 2) my heart is a garden. The more open I become to God and the more I accept the identity He's given me, the more easily He can plant things in my heart.

Although it can be a scary and uncomfortable thing to dig into the depths of your past, God has given us the freedom to dig without fear. That's the beautiful thing about His character. When we open our hearts to God, we don't find fear or shame; we only find more freedom. With our new identity as God's treasure, we're no longer slaves to who our sin tells us we are. We don't have to run from our past. Here's something I wrote in my journal when I read through those verses in Matthew:

"I found a hidden treasure inside my earthen vessel. It has taken something, some time to grow it from a thistle to explode it. But I started to water it and tell it to grow. I wouldn't have known it if I didn't start watering it. But when you find the hidden treasures that were implanted from the Creator, and you see them and honor them and water them until they start to grow and remind them that they matter so, something transpires—fruit by the foot, even when you hear the word 'should.' I should do this, and I should do that. Yet when I surrender the 'shoulds,' I start to think about the 'woulds.' Well, I would do this, and I would do that. And that was that. The 'shoulds' got taken over by the 'woulds.' And I would go on to discover all I was meant to find within the treasure chest called love divine."

When we bring Jesus into our past, into the parts of our story we don't want to tell, He rewrites the narrative. He changes the story. You may have seen it one way before—"He wasn't there. How could this have happened to me if Jesus was with me?"—but when you let Him in, He flips the script.

"I *was* there," He says. "I was there in your darkest moments, right alongside you. I was there, sitting with you, crying with you, carrying you on my shoulders. I've always been there."

When we place our hearts in the hands of the Creator, He gives us a new identity and releases us from our sin and shame. When we give Jesus our ball of light, when we find our worth in Him, He turns it into something so much brighter. And, in the end, we feel a whole lot lighter.

PRAYER

DEAR JESUS, THANK YOU FOR ALWAYS BEING WITH ME, EVEN IN MY DARKEST MOMENTS. THANK YOU FOR MAKING ME YOUR TREASURE. I NO LONGER NEED TO FEAR MY PAST OR SHAME. AMEN.

SCAN THE QR CODE TO HEAR MY SPECIAL PRAYER OVER YOU & LISTEN TO TREASURE HOLDER (SENDINGANDMENDING.COM / TREASURE-HOLDER)

Treasure Holder Lyrics

I ask You a question here
Is it wrong to have this fear
The keys to this chest of gold
Have become too heavy to hold

Place your heart in Mine
I am the Divine
And you are Mine
(x2)

Let Me hold you
Let Me hold you

I am the Treasure Holder
I am the Treasure Holder
I am the Treasure Holder
Let Me hold your heart in Mine
(x2)

The treasure, the treasure
Hold your heart in Mine
(x2)

Now I cast my cares to You
Just like You've said to do
Unlock this heart of mine
To forever trust in Thine

Place your heart in Mine
I am the Divine
And you are Mine
(x2)

You are the Treasure Holder
You are the Treasure Holder
You are the Treasure Holder
Hold this mended heart of mine
(x2)

Thank You for reminding me
That You're inside of me
I will forever be
Your treasure, Your treasure
(x2)

Your treasure, Your treasure

HEART SCRIBE JOURNAL

_____
_____
_____
_____
_____
_____
_____
_____
_____
_____
_____
_____
_____
_____
_____
_____
_____
_____
_____
_____
_____
_____

CHAPTER VI
SINKING SAND

In the middle of a clear April night, I lay on the pavement in my cul-de-sac, staring at the stars.

"God, I don't care how long it takes," I said to the sky. "I'm going to lie here until I see a shooting star."

I couldn't sleep. I was battling deep, heavy grief from news I'd received a few days earlier, and lying in bed that night, it had hit me for the first time. My grandma—who listened to me, who encouraged me, who played with me, who lived beside my parents my whole life—was dying.

This is it, I thought. *This is really happening.*

For the first time since Ben died three years prior, I felt the familiar sting of loss. As I faced the reality of Gram's remaining days, that same helplessness and loneliness took over my mind. Ben wasn't here. Grandma couldn't be, either. Grandma had lived ninety-two years of intentional, Spirit-filled life and had provided one of the most positive influences on my own. She was my *rock*. Now she was deteriorating from pancreatic cancer in front of my eyes. In a few days, I'd lose her forever.

Even after Ben passed away, I thought I had everything together. I thought I was invincible, that I was doing all the right things.

On the surface, that's the persona I gave off. But that's the interesting thing about deep loss. It exposes your *true* self—what's lying underneath the surface—in how you react. The prospect of Grandma's death crashed in front of me and uncovered everything hidden in my soul. It pulled back the curtain. Out of nowhere, I was a little kid again, with no one to protect me. Completely helpless. Sinking without a lifeline.

I couldn't keep myself together. Yes, Grandma still lived and breathed, but I felt the end coming. The following Sunday, I ran into Gram's funeral director, who also happened to be a member of our church. When I saw her, I bawled my eyes out.

"My grandma's dying," I told her. "I feel like something's happening to me. My life is unraveling."

Gram was one of the few people who really *knew* me. She not only understood me—always asking the right questions and listening well—but she also loved me *so well*. She supported me. She encouraged me. She lived alongside me and set an example for how to walk with Jesus. She provided so many things I wasn't finding anywhere else in my life. Now I was just supposed to accept that all of that was going away?

"You're right," the funeral director replied. "Something *is* happening. Your foundation is crumbling."

Now *that* was a word from the Lord. First, Ben; now, Grandma. I was losing pieces of my foundation.

"It's like sinking sand," she continued. "It's crumbling beneath your feet."

Now I was *really* crying.

In that moment, I realized I'd built my foundation on something *good*, yes, but ultimately, something *temporary*. My grandma exemplified hope, joy, and love to me, and as she began her departure from this world, I found myself sinking. I'd relied so heavily on my relationship with Gram that I'd forgotten to plant my feet in the only One who is steady, constant, and *eternal*. I

"

EVERY CREATED THING
IN THIS WORLD IS
TEMPORARY, EVEN
OUR DEEPEST, MOST
MEANINGFUL HUMAN
RELATIONSHIPS. GOD'S
LOVE IS CONSTANT. IT'S
ETERNAL.

anchored my ship to the *gift*, not the Giver.

As I drove back from church—still crying, still losing it—a song from Josh Baldwin, "Stand in Your Love," came on the radio:

> *My fear doesn't stand a chance*
> *When I stand in Your love.*

"Micah, this is your message," God told me.

Again, it hit me like a ton of bricks—bricks I was about to use to build a *new* foundation.

However good or beautiful they may be, we can't build a foundation on things of this world. Our ultimate love cannot be based in the love of people. I couldn't build up my life on the love of my husband or the love of my parents or the love of my grandparents. Although God *used* those people in my life to show me His goodness and His love, ultimately, they were gifts. They were temporary. They were a means of directing me back to the Source, the Giver of those good gifts.

That's the bottom line. Every created thing in this world is temporary, even our deepest, most meaningful human relationships. God's love is constant. It's eternal. Why did I feel helpless? Why did I feel like I was sinking? It was because I rooted my foundation in the love of people—not the love of God—and that love started to fade. Suddenly, I had nothing on which to stand.

Two days before Grandma left this world, my helplessness reached a peak. When I walked into her room that afternoon, I found her with bruises all over her face and body. She had tripped and fallen earlier that morning. No one gave me a heads up about what had happened—probably knowing full well how I'd react—and seeing Grandma in that state pushed me over the edge. That was it. I was done. I left the house and started pacing outside. I'm not a panicked person, but in that moment, I felt myself on the verge of a panic attack. All of this was just too much, too real.

In my finite, human perspective—on my foundation of temporary, created things—I saw my life through a lens of loss. *Where are You, God? Why are You doing this to me?* I'd been standing on a less-than-firm foundation, and I could only see what I was losing. I focused exclusively on the ground crumbling beneath my feet. But even in my vulnerability, God showed me His true character. He showed me His love, His gentleness, and His grace. He shifted my focus away from what I was *losing* and toward what I was *gaining*: a true, firm, lasting foundation in Him and His goodness.

His loving-kindness was all around us in those final days. Just hours before I'd walked in to see Gram covered in bruises—on that Wednesday before she passed—my sister showed up, too. Without prior communication, we arrived just *hours* apart. In the middle of a global pandemic—a time when she could've been isolated in a lonely hospital room—Gram got to be at home, surrounded by her family. Grandma didn't call anyone to her side, but God *drew* us to her. That same day, we sang "The Blessing" by Kari Jobe over her together:

> *May His favor be upon you*
> *And a thousand generations*
> *And your family and your children*
> *And their children, and their children*

In His grace, God drew four generations of women to be there on one of Grandma's last days of life. Her daughter-in-law and daughter (my mom and my aunt), her granddaughters (my sister and me), and her great-granddaughters (my daughter and my niece) all sang over Grandma that morning. The Father gave us one last gift on Gram's behalf before He took her home.

The next day, another friend from our church—whose grandma

"

IN THE PRESENCE OF THE LORD, THERE IS FREEDOM. THERE IS LIBERTY.

also lived in that neighborhood—drove by my grandma's house where we'd sung. When she did, guess what song came on her radio?

"The Blessing."

For most of April, I had focused on the loss. That whole month, it stung. People in my life were dying, and they couldn't be replaced. I kept asking myself, "How can I go on with my life without Grandma and Ben?" Loss is a very difficult thing to accept.

But that wasn't the end of the story. Death isn't a surprise to our Creator. It doesn't thwart His good plan. He already *defeated* death, and because of that, He *uses* things like death and loss for *good* (see Genesis 50:20). From His eternal perspective, even in death, there is still His goodness, mercy, and grace. When we take on that eternal perspective ourselves, we begin to see the *gains* instead of just the losses. We set our feet on a firm, unchanging foundation.

As I held Grandma's hand before she died, surrounded by four generations of women singing together, God put a different song on my heart. My insides are all lyrics—it's just how God speaks to me—and an old hymn came rushing into my mind:

> *I can run through a troop*
> *And leap over a wall.*
> *Hallelujah, Hallelujah.*
> *Now I'm free from condemnation,*
> *Jesus is the Rock of my salvation.*

In that moment, God showed me His perspective.

"Leap, Grandma!" I said quietly as she slept. "You can go. Leap over the wall of death, Grandma."

In the presence of the Lord, there is freedom. There is liberty. I don't know about you, but when I worship, I can't sit still. I understand different people have different expressions of worship, but when I'm in God's presence, I'm all over the place. I'm jumping and dancing and moving. And in that moment, I knew Grandma was entering that freedom, running wild and free with her Creator in eternity.

At 5:00 a.m. on Friday, May 1, 2020, with my aunt holding her hand, Grandma left this world for eternity. On the first day of the fifth month, God gave her the grace to go, to leap over the wall. My aunt passed Grandma's hand into the hand of her Creator, and He took her into the Promised Land, where there was no more sinking sand. She didn't go alone—she leapt over that wall of death with her Father—and now she's running wild and free.

God is kind. God is merciful. God is near. Yes, death is difficult to understand. Loss is really hard. It often feels unfair. It doesn't make sense. But it's not about, "Why do bad things happen to good people?" It's about God's *goodness*. It's about what He wants to show us, what He wants to give us in the *middle* of our pain. He wants to shape us, to grow us, to make us into the people He's always meant for us to be. He promises us *life*—all He asks in return is for us to see things through His eyes.

After "Sinking Sand," I wrote another song, also related to my grandma's passing. It doesn't have a title (yet), and it might not ever be published, but I wrote it through the lens of what Grandma must be seeing now in heaven:

> *Oh, Your face is beaming at me*
> *And I can't wait to see*
> *Oh, Your face is beaming at me*
> *With glee*
> *And now I see You in me*
>
> *Now I see*
> *It's You and me*
> *Walking into eternity*
> *Now I can see*

I's always been You and me
As we're walking into eternity
Oh, now I can see Your face
Is looking back at me
As we're walking into eternity

Back in my cul-de-sac, on that clear April night, God showed up. After about thirty minutes of waiting, a shooting star shot across the sky. Then another. Then another. Even before Gram died, God showed me His presence, how He's always been with me, how He's been the One behind every good gift in my life. I was covered. I was safe. My Creator was looking down on me.

"OK, God," I told Him. "I see You."

PRAYER

DEAR JESUS, HELP ME TO STAND FIRM ON YOUR WORD, EVEN WHEN LIFE IS HARD AND DOESN'T MAKE SENSE. YOU ALONE ARE MY FIRM FOUNDATION. AMEN.

 SCAN THE QR CODE TO HEAR MY SPECIAL PRAYER OVER YOU & LISTEN TO SINKING SAND
(SENDINGANDMENDING.COM/SINKING-SAND)

Sinking Sand Lyrics

A kiss on the hand
Takes her to another land
A touch from her man
Helps her build a bridge over sinking sand

He wants to hold her hand
He never wants to leave
He wants to take her back
Back to that promised land

Where His mercy kiss is all she needs
It helps her to be free
She finally believes He's all she needs
That mercy kiss is blessed from Thee

Just one kiss on the hand brings her back
to that land
Just one kiss on the hand brings her back
to that land

Back to that promised land
Where there's no sinking sand

He wants to hold her hand
And take her to that promised land

Where His mercy kiss is all she needs
It helps her to be free
She finally believes He's all she needs
That mercy kiss is blessed from Thee

Just one kiss on the hand brings her back
to that land
Just one kiss on the hand brings her back
to that land

It all started with a kiss on the hand
Oh, how I know that kiss
That I'll always miss
It connects me to Thee
Now I feel so free

Oh, it connects me to Thee
Now I feel so free

It all started with a kiss on the hand
(x4)

HEART SCRIBE JOURNAL

CHAPTER VII
RAYS

I love nature. I'm a firm believer that God speaks through His creation—shooting stars, sunsets, rainbows. It's always sending a message.

In the aftermath of Ben's death, I felt God awaken me to His creation. I became more in tune with the squirrels scurrying, the bunnies hopping, the birds singing their melodies, so I started asking God for more—for proof He was near.

Since Ben's passing, every June, lightning bugs have filled the woods in my backyard. And not just low-flying, low-energy, run-of-the-mill fireflies. These things light up my backyard—from the grass to the tops of the trees. That never happened before—and every year, it feels like an anniversary gift. I believe it's Yahweh reminding me that I am loved and that I am never alone. He opened my eyes to all of it, to the beauty of His loving-kindness all around me. He gave me a renewed gratitude for His creation.

Sometimes, I'll even chase it. I'll be having a bad day, but suddenly, the rain will come. And the light will start peeking through the clouds. Then I'll know.

There's a rainbow out there somewhere. Time to go find it.

I know it sounds silly to drive several miles to find even the faintest rainbow across the sky, but every time, it's been worth it.

On a family trip to Nags Head, North Carolina, I went chasing again—this time, for that beautiful North Carolina sunset. I wanted to take advantage of my time on the coast, to really embrace the ocean while I was down there. The sun took it from there.

As I pulled up to the beach, I saw it. Just beyond a layer of receding clouds, the multicolored sunset stretched across the sky, leaving no corner of the horizon unpainted by its orange, yellow, and purple hues. The rays beamed out in every direction, drawing beautiful patterns in their farewell to another day.

Standing there watching, consumed by the beauty around me, I got this little line:

> *No matter the days*
> *You keep sending down Your rays*

I didn't *have* to see the sunset on that summer night. I could've stayed inside. I could've sat on my phone all day and let the day pass into night without looking up. Plenty of the Nags Head residents—out of habit, routine, or just "more important" things—chose that path. Still, the sunset came. The beach still called. He still sent down His rays.

Every season, every day, every *moment*, God gives us a choice. Because He is constant—because His loving-kindness *always* surrounds us—He's not the dependent variable in the equation of our life. It's on *us*. When our circumstances turn against us, we have a choice whether we're still going to praise Him—whether we're still going to bask in His rays—or curse Him. No matter the day—good, bad, or in-between—He continues to show up. He continues to be faithful. He continues to send down His rays. The rest is up to us.

Are we going to lift up our praise? Will we still do it when our circumstances beat us down? When we've lost our job? When our family members die? When we're going through a divorce?

Victim or victor—ultimately, it's our choice. Yahweh has already given us our identity as His children, as victors and coheirs with Christ. Will we throw that all away in the face of difficult circumstances? Or will we continue lifting up our praise, no matter the days?

In September 2020, my heart felt heavy thinking about Ben's death. To help me process, I pulled out my journal and had a conversation with the Holy Spirit:

> *"Why is my heart feeling this way?" I wrote.*

> *"When your heart gets too heavy, it takes you to the grief levy," came the response.*

> *"This levy, how long must he (Ben) be a part of my being? He left me."*

> *"It was time, Micah. He ran his race."*

> *"Why?"*

> *"In time, you will understand more of the eternal story. When your hurt is burning, your heart is discerning."*

> *"So why is it burning? Who is it burning for?"*

> *"Your heart is burning for an open door into the land of the more."*

> *"Why am I burning? What do You want to reveal to me, Jesus?"*

"

WHEN OUR
CIRCUMSTANCES TURN
AGAINST US, WE HAVE A
CHOICE WHETHER WE'RE
STILL GOING TO PRAISE
HIM—WHETHER WE'RE
STILL GOING TO BASK IN
HIS RAYS—OR CURSE HIM.

"I want to show you the way to walk out of trauma into my happy place called an eternal space. This eternal space is a way to connect to the realm where true peace, healing, anointing, deep feelings, gentleness, and kindness all spring forth. When you tap into the garden of the heart, you connect to My garden, to My Eden within. Within you, Eden is available."

"What can I glean from there? What do You want me to see?"

"My city called eternity. The land flowing with milk and honey. This coating of goodness and the sweetness of words has landed you in Eden, the paradise at the beginning. There was bliss, pleasure, fruit, and dominion there. Creativity was active, and walking with me was daily. It was so intimate. But Adam and Eve wanted more. They were tricked and got bitten by the 'I can do it' pride viper. Pride hides. Pride lies. Pride never wants the flesh to die. Pride can't see the truth of abiding in me. Pride blinds."

"Why are You revealing this?" I responded.

"Because it's time to let go of the pride that says, 'I know.' Stop holding on. Let go of 'I know' into the unknown. I do know, and it's not unknown. Pride is blocking you more than you know."

"Pride in what areas? Where am I still blinded?"

"Like Leah and Jacob—that producing things buys the love."

At the time, I was reading through Genesis 29, the story of Jacob, Leah, and Rachel. Laban, Rachel and Leah's father, tricks Jacob into marrying Leah, the older sister, yet Jacob wants Rachel. In the end, Jacob ends up working a total of fourteen years for Laban to marry two different wives. Naturally, this leads to some conflict.

Jacob loves Rachel. Leah feels neglected. Yahweh sees Leah in her pain and has compassion on her:

> *"When Yahweh saw that Leah was unloved, he opened her womb, but Rachel remained childless."*
> (Genesis 29:31, TPT)

Leah, though, takes God's gift and twists it.

Verse 32 says, "Leah conceived, gave birth to a son, and named him Reuben, saying, 'Because Yahweh looked upon me with compassion in my misery, surely, my husband will love me now!'"

Surely, my husband will love me now.

Leah tried to turn God's gift into a means of false fulfillment. She had her path to happiness and identity mapped out—"earn the love of my husband." And, thanks to the goodness of God, she finally had a means of getting there—or so she thought. But, as the children kept coming for Leah, the pattern of pride, hope, and disappointment continued.

Verses 33 and 34 continue the story: "She conceived again, gave birth to a son, and named him Simeon, saying, 'Yahweh has heard that I am despised, and in his mercy, he gave me this son also.' Leah conceived the third time, gave birth to a son, and named him Levi, saying, 'This time my husband will be joined to me, because now I've given him three sons!'"

God saw Leah in her pain, loneliness, and heartache. His loving, compassionate nature is drawn to the hurting. The mercy in His heart is touched by the poor, broken, and rejected. But Leah couldn't understand the *depth* of how greatly the Lord loved her.

Pride blocked it, hid it. Pride lied to Leah and convinced her that she still knew what was best, that she could find true fulfillment and identity outside God's love.

"This time my husband will be joined to me..."

Can you see the desperation and longing there?

Pregnancy after pregnancy, child after child, Leah kept waiting for Jacob's love, expecting him to love her, trying to *earn* his love.

"After Reuben, he'll love me."

"After Simeon, he'll love me."

"After Levi, he'll love me."

Pride is a blocker—it kept Leah in a performance state. As a woman of her time and culture, Leah's honor came from fertility. Her worth was attached to producing children. That was her leverage, her means of earning Jacob's love.

That was *me*. I was Leah. Through all these different identities I'd put on—wife, mother, worship leader, real estate agent—I tried to earn the love of God and the people around me.

If I do this, people will love me. If I do this, God will love me, too. But if I don't, I'm on my own.

By the grace of God, Leah's story didn't end with Levi—and neither did mine.

"Once again, Leah conceived and gave birth to a son. She named him Judah, saying, 'This time I will praise the Lord!'"

This time I will praise the Lord.

The TPT footnote for that verse, Genesis 29:35, says this:

> "Over the years of struggling with the pain of being unloved, Leah finally opened her heart to the Lord, and grace touched her. God was tenderly wooing her to himself through her disappointment in her marriage. At last, she gives birth to her fourth son and resolves to praise the Lord no matter what. *Leah has now become a worshipper of the Almighty.*"

How incredible is that?

No matter what.

Yahweh is *good*, people! Leah spent *years* struggling with her identity, and throughout *all of it*, Yahweh remained good. He kept loving Leah. He kept opening doors and giving her opportunities. Despite her pride, despite her stubbornness and unwillingness to come outside and bask in His sunset, He kept sending down His rays. Leah strived all she could, the best way she knew how, to gain Jacob's love, and when she finally surrendered, it wasn't *Jacob's* love that she actually needed.

And look where she ended up: in the lineage of Jesus Himself.

Gratitude breaks the chains of oppression. When we put a little effort into seeking God's love, He will *always* show up. He will *always* send His rays. All we need to do is surrender. All we need to do is look up.

> *No matter, no matter how it ends*
> *You'll be there, you'll be there till the end*

This time I will praise the Lord.

His loving-kindness is all around us—all the time. Will you chase it?

PRAYER

DEAR JESUS, THANK YOU THAT I DON'T HAVE TO EARN YOUR LOVE. YOU CONTINUE TO LOVE ME DESPITE MY FAILURES AND SEND DOWN YOUR RAYS IN LAYERS OF GOODNESS EVERY DAY. AMEN.

SCAN THE QR CODE TO HEAR MY SPECIAL PRAYER OVER YOU & LISTEN TO RAYS
(SENDINGANDMENDING.COM/RAYS)

Rays Lyrics

No matter the day
God wants to show you a way
Not just a way, but a brighter way

You see the truth and the light
This light is shown in a ray
To power your day and to show you His might

For a brighter day
Step out and see
The rays of God's glory
(x2)

No matter the days
You keep sending down Your rays
And I'll keep lifting up my praises
No matter what the day says
(x2)

So, daughters of light
It's time to carry His might

Step outside and look into the light

For we are walking by faith
And not by sight
Cause we are daughters of light and we carry
His might

For this is the choice
To raise our voice
With the weight of God's glory
(x2)

No matter the days
You keep sending down Your rays
And I'll keep lifting up my praises
Until the final day ends
(x2)

No matter, no matter how it ends
You said You'll be there, You'll be there till the end

Hope for tomorrow is not in your day
It comes down through the rays

HEART SCRIBE JOURNAL

_____
_____
_____
_____
_____
_____
_____
_____
_____
_____
_____
_____
_____
_____
_____
_____
_____
_____
_____
_____

CHAPTER VIII
KEY

As I continue this journey of knowing the Father's heart, I've noticed a pattern. As my understanding of Yahweh deepens, I've seen a progression—from *knowledge* to *relationship* to *intimacy*. Let's take a look at each of these concepts.

1. Knowledge

With the help of the Holy Spirit, *knowledge* is the starting point of any human relationship with God—it's a recognition and initial understanding of who Yahweh is, what He's done, and what He continues to do. I love how David describes this in Psalm 139—in The Passion Translation, of course:

> *"Lord, you know everything there is to know about me.*
> *You perceive every movement of my heart and soul,*
> *and you understand my every thought before it even enters my mind.*
> *You are so intimately aware of me, Lord.*
> *You read my heart like an open book*
> *and you know all the words I'm about to speak*
> *before I even start a sentence!*

*You know every step I will take before my journey even
begins.
You've gone into my future to prepare the way,
and in kindness you follow behind me
to spare me from the harm of my past.
You have laid your hand on me!
This is just too wonderful, deep, and incomprehensible!
Your understanding of me brings me wonder and
strength."
(Psalm 139:1–6)*

The footnote for verse 5 says, "Or, 'You hem me in before and
behind.' The implication is that God protects the psalmist from
what may come in the future and what has happened in the past."
This is where it all starts. When I recognized *who* Yahweh is and
what He's done—not only in the world around me, but in my life,
specifically—I began to move toward Him.

Wait a minute. He's been with me this whole time.

In my limited human knowledge, I don't know what He's saved
me from in my past. I don't know the car accidents I missed or
the angels He sent to protect me. In my human nature, I *assumed*
safety and, for the most part, remained unaware of what God
was doing on my behalf. But that matters! That's huge, people! I
didn't save myself by "being smart" or "planning ahead"—I have
so much less control than I thought. The good news is, though,
His kindness and love protect me. Yahweh is always working on
my behalf:

*"You formed my innermost being, shaping my delicate
inside
and my intricate outside,
and wove them all together in my mother's womb.
I thank you, God, for making me so mysteriously complex!*

"

HE KNIT ME TOGETHER, HE
EMBROIDERED ME WITH
INTENTIONALITY AND
SPECIFICITY.

> *Everything you do is marvelously breathtaking.*
> *It simply amazes me to think about it!*
> **How thoroughly you know me, Lord!"**
> *(Psalm 139:13–14, bold emphasis mine)*

Again, the footnote here is beautiful: "The Hebrew word for 'knit' or 'wove' can also be translated 'covered' or 'defended.' God places an eternal spirit inside the conceived child within the womb of a mother and covers that life, sends the child a guardian angel, and watches over him or her."

His guidance and protection go back farther than I ever even realized. He's been with me from the beginning! He knit me together, He *embroidered* me with intentionality and specificity. When we learn and understand about the *love* and *goodness* of our Creator, how could we *not* move toward Him?

At the end of the chapter, that's just what David does—he turns inward, to his own response:

> *"God, I invite your searching gaze into my heart.*
> *Examine me through and through;*
> *find out everything that may be hidden within me.*
> *Put me to the test and sift through all my anxious cares.*
> *See if there is any path of pain I'm walking on,*
> *and lead me back to your glorious, everlasting way—*
> **the path that brings me back to you."**
> *(Psalm 139:23–24, bold emphasis mine)*

You can just hear the overflowing *gratitude* coming through those last two verses. As David learned more about the Father's heart, he surrendered more of his life over to Yahweh. From there, you can see the trust begin to grow. Instead of, "Oh, I have to go to God with *another* problem. Dad's gonna be so annoyed with me," it's like, "No, this is what He *loves* to do. He *wants* to help me." Gratitude leads to trust, and trust builds relationship. As I began to surrender more to Yahweh, I found myself *wanting* to be in His presence more and more.

2. Relationship

The Apostle John puts words to this next step in the process in his first letter:

> *"So you must be sure to keep the message burning in your hearts; that is, the message of life you heard from the beginning. If you do, you will always be living in close fellowship with the Son and with the Father. And he himself has promised us the never-ending life of the ages to come! I've written these things about those who are attempting to lead you astray. But the wonderful anointing you have received from God is so much greater than their deception and now lives in you. There's no need for anyone to keep teaching you. His anointing teaches you all that you need to know, for it will lead you into truth, not a counterfeit. So just as the anointing has taught you, remain in him."*
> *(1 John 2:24–27, bold emphasis mine)*

I love that word—"burning." In the footnote of the TPT, it says, "Or, 'residing in You.'" As I surrender to Yahweh and allow that corresponding trust to build, my relationship with Him becomes more consistent. As John writes, when this happens, "there's no need for anyone to keep teaching you." In relationship with the Father, filled with His Holy Spirit, we have everything we need. And, in the end, everything's going to be all right.

> I let Him inside of me
> So He can burn to the core of me

"

HIS DESIRES BECOME
MY DESIRES. HIS HEART
BECOMES MY HEART.

Now I feel a warmth inside
That everything going to be alright

3. **Intimacy**

This is where my pursuit of the Father took its final and most significant step—a process that's ongoing and ever-developing: *intimacy*. As I've developed a relationship with the Father more consistently—and sat in His presence more and more—my *desire* for Him began to grow exponentially. His desires became *my* desires. His heart became *my* heart. All I want with my life is to walk in step with Him.

Of course, for expertise on intimacy, I turned to Song of Songs:

> *"**Fasten me upon your heart as a seal of fire forevermore.**
> **This living, consuming flame**
> **will seal you as my prisoner of love.**
> My passion is stronger
> than the chains of death and the grave,
> all consuming as the very flashes of fire
> from the burning heart of God.
> Place this fierce, unrelenting fire over your entire being."*
> *(Song of Songs 8:6, bold emphasis mine)*

Understanding who God is turns into relationship, and this relationship creates a deep-seeded, intense *desire* for more.

Fasten me upon your heart as a seal of fire forevermore.

That's intense language—but it's also based so deeply in love.

This living, consuming flame will seal you as my prisoner of love.

It's an outward reflection of inward intimacy.

This is it, people. *This is the key.*

This is what He's calling us to, ultimately—not just to know *about* Him, but to grow in intimacy *with* Him. As humans, this is exactly how we connect with each other. We may *think* we can connect with others through information and logistics, but at the end of the day, those conversations always leave us feeling empty. It's not enough to share the topical happenings of our lives. We need emotional authenticity. We need to be vulnerable. We need intimacy. A book I read recently, *Connection Codes,* put it like this:

> *"Humans do not connect through logistics. Logistics are the facts and figures, the information, the content... Logistics are real and valid, but they do not connect us relationally. Logistics bring us together geographically; emotions bring us together relationally."* [1]

We can have plenty of conversations with other people throughout our life, but if there's no *heart* in those conversations, there will be no intimacy. We'll walk away feeling empty. If we keep God at a distance—learning *about* Him without surrendering *to* Him—we'll miss out on the feast! We'll miss out on life itself.

Like any relationship, our relationship with the Father is a process—it's a progression from *knowledge* to *relationship* to *intimacy*. But unlike most human relationships, Yahweh won't let us down. As we grow closer and closer to Him, we can have confidence that our hope won't return void.

> Let him pull you through
> It's what He loves to do

In the end, there is a burning—but it's not to hurt us. We're not the victims of the fire. We are the *victors*. It's a refining fire

---

1. Dr. Glenn and Phyllis Hill and Echo Hill-Vetter, *The Connection Codes: The Blueprint & Tools for Creating the Relationships You Crave* (independently published, 2021), 57.

to remove the layers and bring us closer to Yahweh. The burning may hurt at times, but we know how this Kingdom story ends. The burning sears a stamp of identity on our hearts, producing a truer outward reflection of His love to others. It's a divine sense of urgency to connect with others and spread the Good News. It doesn't burn to hurt you. It burns to heal you. When the work is done, one thing is for sure: our longing for belonging will be complete.

PRAYER

DEAR JESUS, THANK YOU FOR KNOWING ME INTIMATELY. MAY YOUR DESIRE BECOME MY DESIRES AND YOUR HEARTBEAT BECOME MY HEARTBEAT. I WANT MY LIFE TO WALK IN STEP WITH YOURS. AMEN.

 SCAN THE QR CODE TO HEAR MY SPECIAL PRAYER OVER YOU & LISTEN TO KEY (SENDINGANDMENDING.COM/KEY)

Key Lyrics

Thank You, Lord
For saving me before
All those trials You've brought me through
And the ones that I never knew

You knew me before I knew You
You saw me before I saw me too
You breathed in me and I breathed in You
No matter what I do, my heart burns for You

Thank You, Lord
For saving me before
All those trials You've brought me through
And the ones that I never knew

I let Him inside of me
So He can burn to the core of me
Now I feel a warmth inside
That everything gonna be alright

He is inside of you
So let Him burn through for you

Now I hope you feel the warmth inside
It's a key to your victory

So let Him burn
Let Him burn
Through for you

Let Him burn
Let Him burn
Through for you

Let it go
So He can blow
Through for you

Let Him pull you through
It's what He loves to do
(x2)

We say, Thank You, Lord
For saving me before
And all those trials You've brought me through
And the ones that I never knew

And the ones that I never knew

HEART SCRIBE JOURNAL

CHAPTER IX
BELLS

There's something real God-like about a good nap on a Sunday afternoon. I know Yahweh works in many mysterious ways, but one of the ways *must* be through Sunday naps. I'm convinced.

After one particularly rejuvenating Sunday-afternoon nap, I woke up with this renewed *energy*—Holy Spirit energy. Before I even lifted my head off the pillow, I had lyrics in my brain:

> *I will get up*
> *And honor the King*
> *As I rise up*
> *And sing for Thee*
> *I will get up*
> *And honor the King of Glory*

Here's the reality: many of us are tired of going to church. We're tired. Obviously, there are exceptions to the rule—this isn't meant to be knock against any specific church—but so much of church culture today is just *tired*. The mechanics—the practices, the principles, the process—have stolen our passion for worship. It's tired, and it's *tiring*. We're driven by routine instead of genuine desire. We've grown weary in well doing.

When the COVID-19 pandemic hit, it woke some of us up to this reality—it brought us to a crisis of belief. Many of us did *better* with virtual church than we did gathered in person. It pulled us back and forced us to ask questions that, out of routine and habit, we'd ignored for years:

What do we actually *believe?*

Why do we attend church? Is church more than just an events place anymore? I'm not talking about the purpose of the big-C Church *body*, but why do we, as followers of Jesus, choose to gather every Sunday morning for worship, prayer, and preaching?

> *We will rise*
> *Rise up and honor the King*
> *We will rise*
> *Rise in His victory*
> *We will rise*
> *Rise up and honor the King*

Children of God, have we lost something?

In many ways, church has taken on the identity of our Western culture—consumer-focused, contingency-based, instant gratification. I've heard things like, "How can you keep going to church when things are like this?" or "I'm not getting anything from the pastor. How can you keep coming?" Instead of attending church to *give*, we've flipped the script—we're now going to *get*.

I need a good word from the pastor today.

I need to catch up with my friends before the service.

I need an emotional revival during worship.

We've taken the original intent of gathering and twisted it to match the rest of American life. Instead of going directly to the *Source* for our nourishment—the Father of Light—we're settling for second-day bread. We're looking for meaty sermons from our

"

CHURCH ARISES OUT
OF SEEKING THE LORD
SO MUCH IN OUR DAILY
LIVES THAT WE'RE
OVERFLOWING WITH HIS
GRACE AND LOVING-
KINDNESS—THAT WE
CAN'T HELP BUT SHARE IT
WITH OTHERS.

pastors. We're searching out lively, engaging worship from our musicians. In many ways, we've made ourselves the center of the church, so, naturally, when those things start to fall apart—our friends leave, a pastor retires, the worship style changes—we pack up and head out.

Is this what church gatherings were meant to look like?

So we will rise
And stand up and sing
Praise to our King
He is our victory

When writing this song ("Bells"), two verses came to mind: "Rise up and put your might on display! By your strength we will sing and praise your glorious power!" (Ps. 21:13, TPT).

And this one: "Honor all people. Love the brotherhood. Fear God. Honor the king" (1 Peter 2:17, NKJV).

To me, this is church. This is the Church gathered. Honor all people. Love the brotherhood. Fear God. Honor the King. Sing and praise His glorious power. It's giving instead of getting. Church arises out of seeking the Lord so much in our daily lives that we're overflowing with His grace and loving-kindness—that we can't *help* but share it with others.

After one Wednesday-night worship service, a church member came up to me and said, "Man, coming in here, I wasn't doing good. But I feel better now."

That's the church. It's strength in numbers. There's something spiritual, something invisible that happens to help us break off the chains that so easily ensnare us—the chains of living in the world. Church reminds us that although we're *in* the world, we're not *of* the world. Or, as Pastor Fred Gorini likes to say, "We're spirit beings living in our Earth suits."

There's an old Keith Green song I love, orginally written by

"

YAHWEH IS THE REASON
WE GATHER—EVERYTHING
ELSE IS AN ADD-ON.

Annie Herring, called the "Easter Song," that I think speaks to this true spirit of church gathering:

> *Hear the bells ringing, they're singing*
> *That you can be born again*
> *Hear the bells ringing, they're singing*
> *Christ is risen from the dead*

And then later, in the second verse:

> *Hear the bells ringing, they're singing*
> *That you can be healed right now*
> *Hear the bells ringing, they're singing*
> *Christ, He will reveal it now*

I *love* that! What if that became our reality again? What if we were *excited* to get up for church every morning? What if we *anticipated* the gathering—not necessarily to chat with our friends or be entertained by good worship and preaching, but to *honor the King*?

Kingdom Kids, let's remember who we are. Let's go back to the main point of church. Let's reorient ourselves to the One at the center of everything we do as the big-C Church body. The pastor isn't the point. The worship isn't the point. The preaching isn't the point. *He* is the point. Yahweh is the reason we gather—everything else is an add-on. We come to honor the King:

> *Oh, I hear the bells ringing*
> *As we're singing*
> *The victory song*
> *Sung all the day long*

PRAYER

DEAR JESUS, PUT INTO ME A PASSION AND EXCITEMENT TO GO TO CHURCH AND BE WITH YOUR PEOPLE ON THE LORD'S DAY! YOU ARE THE REASON WE GATHER, TO CORPORATELY BRING OUR OFFERINGS OF PRAISES TO YOUR HOLY NAME! AMEN.

 SCAN THE QR CODE TO HEAR MY SPECIAL PRAYER OVER YOU & LISTEN TO BELLS (SENDINGANDMENDING.COM/BELLS)

Bells Lyrics

I will get up and honor the King
As I rise up and sing for Thee
I will get up and honor the King of glory

We will get up and honor the King
As we rise up and sing for Thee
We will get up and honor the King of glory

We will rise, rise up and honor the King
We will rise, rise in His victory

We will rise, rise up and honor the King
We will rise, rise in His victory
Rise in His victory

Yeah, let it rise
Let it rise

So, we will rise
Rise up and sing

Praise to our King
He is our victory

So, we will rise
Stand up and sing
Praise to our King
He is our victory

Oh, I hear the bells ringing
As we're singing
A victory song
Sung all the day long
(x2)

We will rise, rise up and honor the King
We will rise, rise in His victory

We will rise, rise up and honor the King
We will rise, rise in His victory
Rise in His victory

HEART SCRIBE JOURNAL

CHAPTER X
DOVE

Out of the blue one day—I wish I could remember the context, but I don't—I received this text from Christine, a friend of mine:

"God's fire is my desire. I will beat this lame heat and rise above and fly like a dove. Ain't no more playing around. I can't be the devil's clown. God's coming back to town, and I need to be ready to wear His gown!"

Boom!

That hit me hard. It stopped me in my tracks.

Well, something's about to go down here.

We hadn't been texting long—that's one thing I *do* remember—but that one response gave me all the insight I needed to understand my friend's heart. I could feel her angst—she didn't want to lose her friends and family for eternity. She was sick and tired of meaningless arguments and hopeless pursuits. She wanted to *go*. She wanted to *move*. She wanted to *get ready* because Jesus is coming back.

Let me tell you—that woke something up in me.

Yes! She's right. We need to go, people! This is who we are.

Throughout the Bible, we see imagery of soldiers, armor, and battle. We're called to "put on the full armor of God" (Eph. 6:11, NIV). We're told God goes before us *and* will "be our rear guard" (Isa. 52:12, NIV). Paul tells Timothy to "overcome every form of evil as a victorious soldier of Jesus the Anointed One. For every soldier called to active duty must divorce himself from the distractions of this world so that he may fully satisfy the one who chose him" (2 Tim. 2:3–4, TPT).

This is our identity as the Body of Christ. This is our position— to stand and declare that God's fire is our desire. We can't play around anymore—people are living in darkness, souls are being lost, the devil is trapping individuals every day. What are we doing? Shouldn't there be a *fire* within our souls?

I'm not talking about "fire" in the negative sense. Forget about God's rage or "fire and brimstone" or the heat of hell. God doesn't motivate His people through fear. God's fire *purifies*. Yahweh is the *Refiner*, like the song written by Chandler Moore from Maverick City Music:

> *I wanna be tried by fire*
> *Purified*
> *You take whatever You desire*
> *Lord here's my life*

God's fire takes my unholiness and makes it holy. It burns off the impurity. To me, *this* is revival. Not that there isn't or wasn't a place for the Billy Grahams and tent revivalists of the world, but for true *revival* to happen, the change needs to start in each one of us. A revival is not a *movement*, per se; it's a collective of individual postures, empowered by the fire of the Holy Spirit, coming together to do radical things.

I feel the Father trying to purify His Church, to bring us back to the grassroots of Acts 2—I feel that deeply within my soul. And

"

WE WEREN'T CREATED
FOR TEMPORARY FLAMES.
WE WERE MADE FOR
GOD'S FIRE.

---

it's coming from a different posture than the tent revivals—it's not based in fear. It's not fear-driven salvation. It's a revival of His *love*. His loving-kindness and mercy are *all around us*, y'all. It's why Jesus died on the cross—because He loved us. The magnitude of His love melts away everything else.

I just want to sound the alarm. Like the end of "Bells"—"I can hear the bells ringing"—I can hear the sound of salvation every day. Wherever we go, we're surrounded by souls desperately in need of the mercy, love, and hope of Jesus. It's so easy to walk around numb—to rush through our days, completely consumed with our "to-do" lists or insecurities or attempts to prove ourselves to the world. But someone in tune with the Father walks a little bit differently. Their movement isn't rushed; it's steady. We're made to be present, to connect to our surroundings. Just look at the life of Jesus—He may have acted *quickly*, but He never *rushed*. Presence and connection defined His time on this Earth.

Really, that's what I keep coming back to—that's what everything *has to* come back to: the Source. Look at the lyrics from "Defender" by Steffany Gretzinger with Rita Springer and John-Paul Gentile:

> *And all I did was praise*
> *All I did was worship*
> *All I did was bow down*
> *All I did was stay still*

This isn't on us; it's on *Him*. We don't have to strive. We don't have to complete religious tasks. All we need to do is make room for the King—to break down the barriers, to allow the Father to strip back the layers we've created in our lives for protection. It's a posture of *being*, letting go, dying to self, and trusting the Father with everything we are.

In one of his sermons, my brother-in-law and pastor, Danny Dillon, used the analogy of a match. On its own, a single match lasts only so long. It burns out quickly. But put ten, twenty, or one hundred matches *together*, and not only will the flame *last longer*; it will also climb higher. Its strength and reach will increase. Together, there's more heat. There's more power. There's more sustainability. Not only that, but "wherever two or three come together in honor of my name, I am right there with them!" Fear tells us, "You're on your own," but Yahweh says, "You're surrounded."

It's time to rise up. It's time for us to get off our butts and stop being complacent. The effects of God's fire looks different in every person—I'm not saying every person should go door-to-door giving out tracts—but that's not up to us. Our job is to stay obedient, let the Father work, and keep plugging into the Source. That is who we are. We weren't created for temporary flames. We were made for God's fire.

Our spirits were made to rise above
Our spirits were made to fly like a dove

PRAYER

DEAR JESUS, KEEP YOUR FIRE BURNING IN ME. FULFILL YOUR WORK THROUGH ME. MAKE MY SPIRIT FLY LIKE A DOVE WITH YOUR MESSAGE FROM ABOVE. AMEN.

SCAN THE QR CODE TO HEAR MY SPECIAL PRAYER OVER YOU & LISTEN TO DOVE
(SENDINGANDMENDING.COM/DOVE)

Dove Lyrics

There ain't no playing around
You're in my home town
(x2)

I'm not the devil's clown
God's coming back to town
(x2)

I need to be ready to wear
His gown when I get up there

God's fire is my desire
God's fire is my desire

I feel the heat of revival fire
I feel the heat of revival fire

No, I won't back down
You can't attack my town

There ain't no playing around
You're in my home town
(x2)

It's time to sound the alarm
God's coming back to town
(x2)

I need to be ready to wear
His battle gear out there

God's fire is my desire
God's fire is my desire

I feel the heat of revival fire
I feel the heat of revival fire

No, I won't back down
You can't attack my town

We must go, we must go and bring them home
And, bring them home
(x2)

Our spirits were made to rise above
Our spirits were made to fly like a dove
(x4)

God's fire is my desire
God's fire is my desire

I feel the heat of revival fire
I feel the heat of revival fire

No, I won't back down
You can't attack my town

HEART SCRIBE JOURNAL

CHAPTER XI
PSALM 23

"The Lord is my shepherd; I shall not want. He makes me to lie down in green pastures; He leads me beside the still waters. He restores my soul; He leads me in the paths of righteousness For His name's sake. Yea, though I walk through the valley of the shadow of death, I will fear no evil; For You are with me; Your rod and Your staff, they comfort me. You prepare a table before me in the presence of my enemies; You anoint my head with oil; My cup runs over. Surely goodness and mercy shall follow me All the days of my life; And I will dwell in the house of the Lord Forever."
(Psalm 139:1–6, NKJV)

On a Sunday afternoon in January 2021, I sat at Don Pancho's Cantina in Franklin, Virginia, with Stone, Stella, Makenzie, and Randolph. Makenzie and Randolph are the daughter and father, respectively, of my childhood best friend, Holly. While we were eating, Randolph got a call from Holly.

Derrick, Holly's husband of twelve years, had tested positive for COVID-19.

I had multiple loved ones battling the physical effects of the pandemic during that early part of 2021, so at the time, I already had several prayer chains in full swing. I wasn't ready for these people to go—I didn't think it was their time—but what else could I do? What else could I do for these people except cry out to Yahweh?

Prayer is all we have.

On Wednesday, Holly called again—Derrick had been moved to the local hospital with low oxygen levels. The next day, Holly tested positive for COVID and had to quarantine at home for two weeks while Derrick quarantined from the hospital. Two weeks later, as Holly finished her quarantine, Derrick took a turn for the worse.

Derrick had underlying health conditions—he was definitely "COVID-conscious"—but still, none of us saw this coming. That Sunday, a week and a half after being admitted to the hospital, Derrick was moved into the ICU. The hospital called Holly—since she wasn't allowed to visit—and told her that if they didn't intubate Derrick, he'd have only a couple days to live.

When we heard the news, our church rallied around Holly, Derrick, and their kids. We started a seventy-two-hour, round-the-clock prayer chain and contended for this family like never before. We prayed for the living God to do a supernatural healing. We prayed for Derrick to stay on this land. It was *go time*, and I was revved up with the Holy Spirit. I was ready to go—so much so that, when I arrived at church that morning for the livestream service, people took notice.

"Why aren't you sad?" they asked me.

I *was* sad, but I was also *energized*. This was an *eternal moment*. I believe we have opportunities to bring the eternal into our everyday lives, and this one was clear. We needed to corporately participate in bringing Heaven to Earth.

We get to turn up. This is what we were made to do. We have an

"

WE GET TO TURN UP.
THIS IS WHAT WE WERE
MADE TO DO. WE HAVE AN
ASSIGNMENT FROM THE
KING.

assignment from the King.

Praying for Derrick, I was perplexed. I had mixed feelings. I'd lived this story out for myself. I was on the other side, and despite how much I missed Ben, I'd seen all the good God had done through my story. I loved Derrick like a brother—I didn't want him to leave—but I also knew how tired he was. He'd seen suicides from friends and family. He'd battled death his whole life—he was born with a sunken breastbone and had his first of three surgeries at age four—and I knew how hard he'd been fighting. I knew how peaceful he'd be with his Father on the other side of death.

Prayer is all we have.

All these people hung in the balance between life and death, and I couldn't control any of it. There was nothing I could do to help Derrick in my earthly, human strength. I *had* to come back to prayer. What else could I do?

God, whatever is Your best, whatever storyline is best, that's what we're asking for Derrick. If that's for him to get healed now, then heal Him, Father. If that's for him to go home to You, then bring him home, Lord.

Ahead of the service, I'd been working on a song based on Psalm 23:

> The Lord is my Shepherd
> I shall not want
> He maketh me lie down
> In the pastures of His heart
>
> He leadeth me beside
> The still waters
> He restores my soul
> He restores my soul

Prayer is our conduit, our connector to the Father. It's stronger than anything else. So often, as humans, we want to use our own human words to pray—and there's a place for that—but there is power in praying the Word of God. When we pray the Word, it activates things because it is *living*. That's how this song came to be—it's based in the belief that when we pray from the Word of God, it activates angelic hosts on assignments. The more we accept our authority to sound the alarms, the more Kingdom activity happens on our behalf. I truly believe that.

I wasn't scheduled to play it that Sunday morning—and I received plenty of opposition—but I felt the Holy Spirit telling me to sing it for Derrick, to dedicate that worship service to him. Despite the obstacles, despite the fact that I hadn't practiced it much, I was gonna sing that song over that man, and he was gonna hear it:

> *Prayer is all I have*
> *Prayer is all I need*
> *When I stop and pray*
> *I can hear you say*
>
> *Stay, please stay*
> *And just pray*

On the livestream, as Derrick watched from his hospital bed, I sang:

> *Will you just stay*
> *Please stay?*

On that Wednesday night, we held a special worship and prayer service for Derrick. Right before it started, Holly told us that, at Derrick's request, the doctors were taking him off the ventilator. They said he wouldn't last long, but we still cried out to God and worshipped. We believed Yahweh could heal Derrick, even

"

HEALING COMES NOT WHEN
GOD GIVES US EVERYTHING
WE THINK WE WANT—
HEALING COMES FROM HIS
PRESENCE.

with how close he was to the next life. Even though we weren't together with him, we got word that Derrick raised his hand during worship. His spirit knew something—I truly believe that.

Most people who walked into worship that night had heavy hearts at the thought of Derrick leaving this Earth. But for me, the Holy Spirit did something different. It was like a light lit up inside me. Coming to terms with my own limitations, to the role I needed to play in *His* bigger plan, gave me peace and freedom. Even though I keeled over, sobbing, when I heard the news, I knew we had an incredible opportunity that night.

I can't control what happens, but I can play my part in what God is doing.

If God was going to take Derrick home that night, I was joining in on what the Holy Spirit was doing. I was going to help usher him into eternity. I was going to praise this saint on over. What a gift! Before the service, I texted this to a friend of mine:

> "We posture our hearts to receive His love. *The sacrifice of praise is something we can only give on this side of eternity. It reveals as it heals,* for the Father is near to a hurting heart. We do our part, and He comes. He always does. He always will. We are *a courageous troop. This, I know.* I love battling and celebrating another faithful member's send-off with you! *Yes, there are tears. Yes, there is sadness.* But joy comes in the morning, through the mourning."

At about 10:45 that night, Derrick crossed over into eternity. He left this world to be with His Father in Heaven. It was a flip on the lyrics of the song.

During that Sunday service, we had humbly pleaded with the Father on behalf of Derrick:

Derrick, will you just stay? Will you please stay?

But Yahweh flipped the script on us. When we come to Him in prayer, when we step into the presence of the Holy Spirit, He says to *us*: "Will you just stay with me? Will you stay and pray? Won't you just stay a little bit longer?"

In our humanity, we want to pull our loved ones back to Earth. We ask God to let them stay here. We think they're better off here, but that's the selfish part of our humanity. What we're *really* saying is, "We won't do better here without you. We don't think life will be better without you here, so we're going to plead with the Father for you to stay."

In our brokenness, we turn God into a *means* instead of an *end*. We want Him to do all these things for us because we don't trust that He's already given us everything we need. Instead of leaning into His unconditional goodness and love, we try to make it conditional: "Father, I'll know you love me *if* you do this thing for me…"

But like He always does, Yahweh flips the script.

Will you just stay, please stay?

Healing comes not when God gives us everything we think we want—healing comes from His *presence*.

> I will fear no evil
> For You are with me now
> You are with me now

Psalm 23:4 summarizes the whole chapter: *"I will fear no evil, for you are with me."*

Andrew Lennon, an artist I follow, put it like this:

> *"Fear comes when we are unaware of the nearness of God. Our awareness that He is with us, His presence, is actually the key to overcoming fear. This is what allows us to walk through the valley of the shadow of death and still*

not be afraid. The lie of fear is simple. It is the belief that God is not with you."

We aren't in control of our lives—or others' lives, for that matter—but that's OK because the only One who is trustworthy *is* in control.

Jesus is all I need
Jesus is all I want
Jesus is my all in all
He is there when I call

Will you just stay
Please stay?

— PRAYER —

DEAR JESUS, THANK YOU FOR BEING NEAR ME, HELPING ME TO OVERCOME MY FEAR. I CAN WALK THROUGH MY DARK DAYS BECAUSE YOU PROMISED TO BE WITH ME, ALWAYS. YOU ARE IN CONTROL OF MY LIFE, AND I CAN PUT MY TRUST IN YOU. AMEN

 SCAN THE QR CODE TO HEAR MY SPECIAL PRAYER OVER YOU & LISTEN TO PSALM 23 (SENDINGANDMENDING.COM/PSALM-23)

Psalm 23 Lyrics

The LORD is my shepherd; I shall not want
He maketh me lie down in the pastures of His heart
He leadeth me beside the still waters
He restores my soul; He restores my soul

He leadeth me in the paths of righteousness
For His name sake, for His name sake
Yea, though I walk through the valley
Of the shadow of death, of the shadow of death

I will fear no evil;
For You are with me now
You are with me now

The Holy Ghost comforts me
And empowers me now,
Empowers me now

Prayer is all I have
Prayer is all I need
When I stop and pray
I can hear You say,
Stay, please stay,
And just pray

Your rod and Your staff, they comfort me
You prepare a table before my enemies
You anoint my head with oil;
My cup overflows, my cup overflows

Surely goodness and mercy
Shall follow me, all of my days
And I will dwell in the house of the LORD
Forever more, forever more

I will fear no evil;
For You are with me now
You are with me now
The Holy Ghost comforts me
And empowers me now,
Empowers me now

Jesus is all I have
Jesus is all I need
Jesus is my all and all
He is there when I call
Will you just, stay, please stay

Yes, I Am the I Am, surrounding you now
(x4)

Will you just stay, please stay
Will you just stay, please stay
Stay, please stay
Will you just stay, please stay
For you are with Me now

Prayer is all we have
Prayer is all we need
When we stop and pray
We can hear You say,
Stay, please stay,
And just pray

Jesus is all we need
Jesus is all we want
Jesus is our all and all
He is there when we call
Will you just, stay, please stay

The LORD is my shepherd; I shall not want
He maketh me to lie down in the pastures of His heart
Will you just stay, please stay

HEART SCRIBE JOURNAL

_____
_____
_____
_____
_____
_____
_____
_____
_____
_____
_____
_____
_____
_____
_____
_____
_____
_____
_____

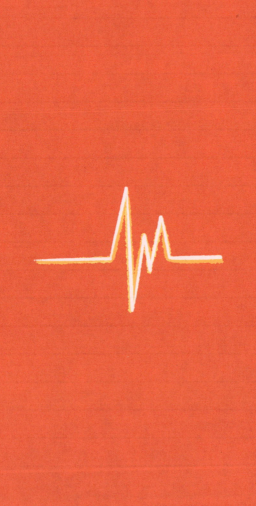

CHAPTER XII
LIFELINE

This chapter is based on Matthew 9:18-22.

She was desperate. How could she not be?

Twelve years.

For twelve years, she'd been like this. Her family, her friends, the doctors—no one could help her. She'd spent all her money on treatments that only made her condition worse. The priests wouldn't go near her. She couldn't worship at the temple. She couldn't participate in society. Her disease and uncleanliness sentenced her to isolation. They defined her. She was alone. Unclean. Dying. Desperate.

Twelve years.

But one day, she heard a rumor—about this man, a teacher from Nazareth, unlike any other rabbi she'd ever heard about or seen. According to the stories, He healed people, even raised them from the dead. He preached of a new Kingdom and forgiveness of sins—not just for the influential and powerful, but for the lonely, lost, and poor. For the desperate.

For those desperate enough to position themselves in uncommon ways. For an unclean woman walking into a crowd of clean people.

At the center of the crowd, she saw a man, hemmed in on all sides, with a prayer shawl over his shoulders.

Could it be?

Could this be that great and merciful Savior, the one who prophet Malachi said had "healing in his wings"? Could this be the Messiah about whom the Law and Prophets spoke?

It doesn't matter. I can't get to Him.

The crowd surrounded Him. He hardly had room to breathe. How could she get to Him? How could she get close enough to ask for healing? She'd have to fight, to push through layers and layers of people—people who'd rejected her, ostracized her, and refused to as much as look at her. Everyone she touched would become unclean; they'd become *like her*. To get to this rabbi, she'd have to risk everything.

Could He really heal me?

She couldn't quiet this growing hope within the depth of her soul. If only she could touch the tassels of His outer garment—surely that would be enough to heal her! Without even looking in her direction, He seemed to be drawing her to Himself.

I know *He can heal me.*

Letting go of her hesitation, she took the first step—toward the center of the crowd, toward the Teacher.

Right away, it was easy. Most people didn't even notice her. Their eyes were fixed on Him, this Jesus of Nazareth. But as she got closer, the crowd began reacting, shouting curses at her as she passed.

"Unclean!" they shouted.

"Stay away!" they cried.

Still, she pushed forward. With every step, she kept her eyes locked on Jesus—the only One who could heal her. To her surprise, people stopped acknowledging her. Something distracted them. She heard shouting. It was Jairus, the Jewish official in charge of the synagogue. He was pleading with Jesus—something about his daughter.

In the commotion, she slipped unnoticed through the crowd. Closer and closer. Finally, she made it to the One she'd been seeking. She could see every detail of the man—the lines on His face, the blue tassels on His shawl, the love in His eyes.

Almost instinctively, her hand stretched out beside her, toward his cloak.

What am I doing? Anyone I touch becomes unclean! How could I do that to this rabbi? How could I infect someone so kind and merciful? How could I keep Him from getting to Jairus's daughter?

Still, her hand reached out. She couldn't contain the faith within the depths of her soul.

If I just touch His clothes, I know *I'll be healed.*

The instant her fingertips touched the edge of his tassels, her bleeding stopped.

Something rushed through her—a power she'd never felt before. *I'm healed.*

As she felt the healing spread throughout her body, giving life to her limbs, she couldn't hold back the laughter bubbling up from within her soul. She hadn't laughed in twelve years!

I'm healed!

Before she could run home and celebrate, a voice pierced through the crowd, sweeping the smile from her face.

"Who touched me?"

It was Him. The rabbi. Jesus. He knew.

"Who touched my clothes?"

If the crowd sees me, they'll kill me. I've defiled a rabbi! They'll pick up stones right now and end me right here!

As the disciples tried to assure Jesus that His question was ridiculous, she felt His presence calling to her again. He pulled her toward Him. Every bone in her body told her to run, to hide until all of this blew over, but she couldn't move. She couldn't stay quiet.

"

THE CROSS WAS THE
GREAT EXCHANGE—THE
ULTIMATE TRANSACTION.

Before she knew what was happening, her body was throwing itself down at Jesus's feet, trembling from head to toe.

"It was me!" she cried. "It was me, rabbi! *I was the one who touched you.* I've been sick—for *twelve years* I've been sick. I heard that You had the power to heal, and so I came—"

He cut her off. He looked her directly in the eyes. She expected scolding, a public condemnation, but His face wasn't angry. All she could see was love.

"Daughter," He said.

Daughter?

"Because you dared to believe, your faith has healed you. Go with peace in your heart and be free from your suffering!"

She couldn't believe her ears. He didn't condemn her. He *healed* her. He *knew* her.

As the crowd once again swept Jesus away, she put her face in her hands—crying, laughing, praying, all at the same time.

Surely, this man is the Messiah. Surely, He is the Son of God.

I've always loved this story. From the first time I heard it—probably back in Sunday school—I loved it, but it wasn't until recently that it hit me in a new way.

When this woman touched Jesus, an *exchange* occurred.

He said to her, "Your faith has healed you."

In exchange for that woman's faith, her trust in Him, Jesus gave her His power. He gave of Himself so that she could be healed—once and for all.

It started with Jesus—His loving-kindness, His magnitude. It drew this woman out like a homing beacon.

I must go.

The closer she got to Jesus, the more she felt *at home.* I truly believe that happened to her. I believe it because it's a reflection of *who Yahweh is*. He calls us to intimacy with Him. It all comes back to that intimacy, y'all! As we step more and more into His presence, we begin to see our true identity more and more clearly.

But the story doesn't stop there. Yahweh respects us enough to not violate our free will. Although He does *draw* us to Himself, He doesn't force us to love Him. He doesn't coerce us into obedience or surrender. Because Yahweh is a loving God, this woman had to make a choice.

Do I seek healing, or do I stay inside? Do I protect myself, or do I go to Jesus?

She could've stayed home. Even in her desperation, going to Jesus was still a *huge* risk for this woman. She had to push against every grain—culture, society, religion, friends, and family—to get through that crowd. She truly had to risk everything she had left to leave her house and go to Jesus—and she did it.

She got out of her house. She pressed through the crowd. She fought her doubts and listened to that still, small voice that said, "I must go." It wasn't religious practice that healed her. It wasn't the doctors or the priests or anything manmade. She had *faith*. Her faith was the transaction.

"Your faith has healed you."

What are we willing to do to get healed, people? What "crowds" are we willing to push through to get close to Jesus, to touch His clothes? Without her choice to leave her house, this woman wouldn't have found healing that day. She wouldn't have encountered Jesus. But because of her choice—because of her *faith*—Jesus restored her.

Jesus honored her faith that day. He didn't have to do anything. The woman did everything by grabbing hold of His hem. But He wanted to *know* her. He wanted a *relationship* with her. He wanted *intimacy* with her. So He invited her to engage with Him.

"Who touched my clothes?"

Jesus already knew the answer to the question, but He wanted the woman to acknowledge her healing. He didn't want their interaction to stop at *physical* restoration. He wanted to *truly, deeply* heal her.

"Go with peace in your heart and be free from your suffering!"

There He was. The same man who'd healed her—what seemed like just a few months before—now hung on a Roman cross. Falsely accused. Convicted. Sentenced to death.

How could this happen?

The man who'd stopped her bleeding now cried out between shallow breaths:

"Father, forgive them."

As the soldiers tied His arms to the crossbeam:

"Father, forgive them."

As the nails pierced His hands:

"Father, forgive them."

As they sorted His clothes and gambled for them:

"Father, forgive them."

Over and over and over. Not, "Please forgive me," but "Father, forgive them."

Along with the crowd of women gathered around her—Jesus's mother and disciples of Jesus like Mary Magdalene—she wept as Jesus struggled for life, gasping for air.

How could they do this to Him?

The One who had saved her, restored her—the One who had *given her life* through His love now sat on death's doorstep, just moments away from His final breath.

Don't they know what they're doing?

Before she looked up, to gaze into His eyes one last time, she

heard Him say again:
  "Father, forgive them."

Was she there that day?

The last time I read through this story, that question hit me: Was this woman, who Jesus had healed just a few chapters earlier, there on the day of His crucifixion? What if she was there? Why wouldn't she have been there?

Obviously, I don't know the full history of the story, but I have to believe that she was there with those women, standing at the foot of the cross, weeping for her Savior. Maybe she knew something the other women and people mourning Jesus didn't know. Because of the exchange she'd experienced earlier, maybe she knew the cross wasn't the end of the story.

> *It is your faith in Me*
> *That will release your healing*
> *I hope you feel His presence*
> *Oh, His healing essence*

Her faith in Jesus released her healing. His presence filled her with His healing essence.

The story of this woman's healing pointed to a greater story Yahweh was already writing—the story of salvation for all people. The cross was the *great* exchange—the ultimate transaction. Jesus gave up *everything* to save us. All He asks for in return is for our faith to be activated. Our trust to be grounded. Our surrender to be led by love.

The bleeding woman had to push through a crowd—through cultural and social obstacles—to get to Jesus. But because of the *cross*, Jesus has made Himself readily available. Father God tore the veil from top to bottom! Through Jesus, He gave us instant access to Himself—for those who believe, who are willing to understand and grow in intimacy with Him.

> *The cross brought you your lifeline*
> *The cross bought you your lifeline*

A faith transaction has an exchange of action. Without the exchange, our lives would never change. Without the great transaction, we would never be able to live with Christ in action.

The cross is our lifeline. The cross puts our lives back in alignment. Can you feel that exchange door opening? If so, go. Run. Push through the crowd, and join the Father in the land of forevermore.

He has been anticipating this day. Don't hesitate! Heaven is waiting to celebrate. Your eternal adventure starts now. Welcome home.

PRAYER

DEAR JESUS, THANK YOU FOR THE CROSS! YOU GAVE UP EVERYTHING TO SAVE ME. THE CROSS BROUGHT ME MY LIFELINE. THE CROSS BOUGHT ME MY LIFELINE. AMEN.

SCAN THE QR CODE TO HEAR MY SPECIAL PRAYER OVER YOU & LISTEN TO LIFELINE
(SENDINGANDMENDING.COM/LIFELINE)

Lifeline Lyrics

When she touched His hem
When she touched His hem

When she touched His hem
She crossed into the promised land
She can feel His presence
Oh, His healing essence
For she said
I knew if I just touched You
I would be healed too
Even by the hem of You

And Jesus said
My beloved
It was your faith in Me
That released your healing
Now go in peace
For you carry a piece of Me
I still feel His presence
Oh, His healing essence

And when I heard the crowd
Shout crucify
I felt an ache inside
That caused me to cry
For He prayed
Over and over
Father, forgive them
For they do not understand

For the cross brought me my lifeline

The cross bought me my lifeline
My lifeline, my lifeline
The cross bought me my lifeline
The cross bought me my lifeline

One thing I know for sure
The cross was my open door
This love was not the finish line
His love was my lifeline

My lifeline
And now I'm walking with the Divine, ohooo

The cross did it
The cross did it
The cross did it
Yes, He finished it

The cross brought you
The cross bought you
The cross longs for you
It's your lifeline

We will sing it again

The cross brought you
The cross bought you
The cross longs for you
It's your lifeline

It is your faith in Me
That will release your healing
I hope you feel His presence
Oh, His healing essence

HEART SCRIBE JOURNAL

_____
_____
_____
_____
_____
_____
_____
_____
_____
_____
_____
_____
_____
_____
_____
_____
_____
_____
_____
_____
_____

WELCOME HOME

WELCOME TO THE
LAND OF THE MORE!

THIS EXCHANGE DOOR
TO THE MORE HAS
BEGUN YOUR NEW LIFE
OF HEART SCRIBING
WITH HIM.

YOUR ADVENTURE AWAITS! LET'S TAKE FLIGHT TOGETHER.

HEART SCRIBE APPAREL

BOOKS BY MICAH N. DILLON

MICAH D
HEART SCRIBE VIBES
AVAILABLE ON ALL DIGITAL PLATFORMS

THE CROSS BROUGHT
        ME MY LIFELINE

YOU'RE NEVER
ALONE

WELCOME HOME

WE WILL RISE IN
    HIS VICTORY